RACE & CLASS

A JOURNAL FOR BLACK AND THIRD WORLD LIBERATION

Volume 42   **January–March 2001**   **Number 3**

Articles appearing in *Race & Class* are abstracted in *Academic Abstracts, Current Contents/Social and Behavioral Sciences, e-Psyche, Historical Abstracts, Multicultural Education Abstracts, SAGE Race Relations Abstracts, Social Science Abstracts* and *Sociological Abstracts*; and indexed in *America: History and Life, British Humanities Index, IBSS, Left Index, Research Alert, Social Science Citation Index, Social SciSearch* and *Social Science Index.*

© Institute of Race Relations 2001

ISSN 0306 3968
ISBN 0 7619 6696 X

Cover design by Arun Kundnani

MARIKA SHERWOOD

Race, empire and education: teaching racism

Quite clearly, virulent anti-Black racism (racial stereotyping, prejudice and discrimination) had its origins in Europe with the trade in enslaved Africans. But there is evidence to indicate that, until the early to mid-nineteenth century, attitudes in Britain towards Black peoples were ambivalent. While many Britons must have benefited from the 'nefarious trade', directly and indirectly, it is quite possible that the majority knew little of it and even less of the racist justifications for enslavement. How – and why – did a racialised view of the world become so widespread in Britain that it became endemic?

This is an attempt to answer that question. I shall argue that, from the mid-nineteenth century, political and commercial developments – the building of an empire and the containment of labour troubles at home, as well as the necessity of providing appropriately lucrative employment for the new middle classes and the younger sons of the nobility – required the institutionalising of an earlier myth of the superior Englishman, now with a civilising mission. It required also the derogation of everyone else into an immutable racial hierarchy whose bottom rung was occupied by Africans. The myth of superiority/ inferiority, held to justify the expropriation of land and the extreme exploitation of labour, was propagated through and by all levels of

Marika Sherwood is the Secretary of the Black and Asian Studies Association and author of many articles and booklets on the history of Black peoples in the UK. Her most recent books are *Kwame Nkrumah: the years abroad, 1935–1947* (Legon, 1996) and *Claudia Jones: a life in exile* (London, 2000)

Race & Class
Copyright © 2001 Institute of Race Relations
Vol. 42(3): 1–28 [0306-3968(200101)42:3; 1–28; 016111]

society and by every available means. It was absolutely necessary for the conquest and settlement of empire and for social cohesion at home.

The sixteenth century

In England and Scotland there was, as yet, no question of empire and very little of education, but Africans were present. Black peoples would have been a relatively common sight in much of southern Europe, because north Africans ruled the Iberian Peninsula for some 700 years and because of trading ventures across the Mediterranean. It is quite possible that some of these Africans ventured north – perhaps those who were adventurous, those who had particular skills and professions scarce in the north and traders. Because of the 'Moors'' renowned scholarship, British scholars must have made their way to the great centres of learning, such as Toledo.[1]

Our earliest written record of Africans in the British Isles comes from the Scottish royal court, where James IV entertained Black ladies and played the part of the Black Knight in tournaments in 1507 and 1508. Luce Morgan (later known as Lucy Negro, the Abbess of Clerkenwell, i.e., a brothel-keeper) was employed by Queen Elizabeth I from 1579 to 1581. There were also Black servants, musicians and skilled workers at the Scottish and English courts and in noble households.[2] There is evidence that some of these servants were paid; the status of others is not known.[3]

There was apparently some confusion about Africans' skin colour at this time. As illustrated in Geoffrey Whitney's poem, 'Impossible', people at first believed that the colour, thought to be a product of tropical climate, could be washed off.[4] There was also bewilderment at the dark-skinned child of an African who was married to 'a faire English woman'.[5] Why did people want to wash off the colour? Because it was strange to them? Perhaps, but there was also an association of the colour black with evil and of white with purity, virginity and virtue. How did these notions interact with the realisation that skin colour is inherent?

In 1555, the merchant John Lok brought a group of Africans to England so that they could learn English and then return to Africa to act as his agents to trade for gold. However, while admitting his need of the services of Africans (and implied in this is his belief that they had the requisite abilities), Lok described them as 'a people of beastly living, without God, laws, religious or common wealth – halfway to purgatory or hell'.[6] This ambivalence is also displayed in the increasing number of published travellers' tales, which mix accurate observation with classical accounts of mythical figures and sheer invention.[7] One would expect Europeans to comment on the differences in appearance, culture, building types and so forth, that they observed between themselves and the people they began to visit on their ocean voyages. But can one call this racist, or is it an inability to grapple with the shock of the new? Or is it possible that Christian dogma made it impossible to see those of other faiths as fully human? What was undoubtedly racist was Lok's description; did he perhaps become an advocate of that equally lucrative trade on the West African coast, the trade in human beings?[8] That not all sixteenth-century voyagers held derogatory attitudes towards Africans has been demonstrated by Paul Hair in a recent article on the subject.[9] However, given the cost of books and the rarity of the ability to read, it is debatable how many in the population would have been influenced by such tales.

Perhaps this sixteenth-century ambivalence towards Africans is best illustrated by two of Shakespeare's plays. (Plays, of course, reached the non-reading public.) In *Titus Andronicus*, first performed in 1595, Aaron, the Black villain, is described as a 'black devil' and takes delight in his evil doings. *Othello* was performed nine years later. The focus of the play is racially motivated sexual jealousy – but Othello is a proud, sensitive, accomplished African, wed to the Duke's (white) daughter. What caused Shakespeare to move from the Black villain to creating the greatest Black literary hero – and to accept that an attractive, aristocratic woman could love an African? Was he initially responding to the fanciful books and the likes of Lok? Had he then met some Africans who made him rethink his prejudices? Or was he in love with the Black woman whom he describes in one of his sonnets (number 130):

> If snow be white, why then her breasts are dun;
> If hairs be wires, black wires grow on her head
> I have seen roses damask'd red and white
> But not such roses see I in her cheeks . . .
> And yet, by heaven, I think my love as rare
> As any she belied with false compare

There are a number of Black villain-heroes in the few surviving Elizabethan plays, portraying a range of attitudes. For example, Thomas Dekker also displays his ambivalence about blackness in his *Lust's Dominion*, probably first performed in 1599. Its hero Eleazor, akin to Aaron, is an evil man. But the Queen, besotted by him, speaks of him as 'the soft-skinned negro'.[10] And Eleazor himself is the mouthpiece for Dekker's ambivalence:

> Black faces may have hearts as white as snow;
> And 'tis the general rule in moral roles,
> The whitest faces have the blackest souls.[11]

The seventeenth century

Even as court ladies were participating in some masques by 'blacking up', and Othello was striding the stage, the Guinea Company was being given its charter (1618) – the company was after gold. More and more Africans were seen in Britain as it became popular to own (or employ) a Black servant. Infinitely more Africans were enslaved and carried to the world that was new to Europeans, some on British vessels.[12]

Whether slavery was legal or not in Britain was debated in the courts from as early as 1569, but the judges could not agree.[13] Advertisements for runaway Blacks (as well as for runaway apprentices) began to appear in the newspapers. Some of the runaways were described as wearing inscribed metal collars – a definite indication of slave status. Other advertisers speak of 'servants'; some give the absconder's name, others do not. Parish registers are equally unclear, most simply giving a name and a physical description, (e.g., 'John Davies, ye black buried' 22 November 1603 at Bisley in Gloucestershire). Only a very few are more informative: for example, 'Williams an Indian slave taken from a boat Bombay in ye east Indies' was baptised 25 September 1687 at Hutton in Essex. What are we to make of this reluctance to ascribe the word 'slave' to runaways or to the baptised or the dead? Is it possible that, while slavery was accepted as an economic necessity in the Americas, there was some uncertainty associated with the holding of slaves in Britain? Did a class differentiation begin to appear? Were the elegantly dressed, even if collared, household servants in Britain, whether servant or slave, seen as different from the field slaves in the Americas? Given recently collected evidence from parish records, it would seem that the free outnumbered the enslaved in England: was this perhaps also seen as a class difference?

New factors now become pertinent to the discussion. The century, which began with the unification of Scotland with England, also witnessed growing Scots and Irish disaffection and the growth of international rivalry between Britain and other European countries: rivalry in India, in Africa, in the Americas. Hence, there arose a need to inculcate nationalism and feelings of superiority not only *vis-à-vis* 'savages' but also more powerful Europeans. With attempts by the monarchy to increase its power, came also a need to emphasise English 'freedom'. A myth about 'freeborn Englishmen', associated with English antiquity and derived from Anglo-Saxon descent and heritage, was assiduously promulgated.[14] Thus began the myth of the Other, always inferior to the English. Daniel Defoe viciously derided this mythmaking in his poem, 'The True-born Englishman' (1701):

The Romans first with Julius Caesar came,
Including all the nations of that name,
Gauls, Greeks, and Lombards, and, by computation,
Auxiliaries or slaves of every nation.
With Hengist, Saxon; Danes with Sueno came . . .
Scots, Picts, and Irish from the Hibernian shore,
And conquering William brought the Normans o'er.
All these their barbarous offspring left behind,
The dregs of armies, they of all mankind;
Blended with Britons, who before were here . . .
From this amphibious ill-born mob began
That vain ill-natured thing, an Englishman.[15]

The eighteenth century

During this century, Britain became the master of the seas and the main exporter of enslaved Africans to the Americas. Canada was ceded to Britain by France; the colonies in North America were lost, while those in the Caribbean became immensely profitable. India, another source of wealth, was administered by the East India Company; the Caribbean colonies generally by their own administrations. (Blacks served in the Royal Navy, the merchant marine and in the military.) Improvements in war, sailing and other technologies, often borrowed or based on developments elsewhere, enabled Europeans to become familiar with (and to exploit) more and more of the world.[16]

Defoe was certainly intellectually excited by these explorations and settlements in the new world. His *Robinson Crusoe*, published in 1719, explores these themes, and the relationship to its inhabitants of the superior Englishman, adrift in this world new to him. But as 'man Friday' is of this new world, he is master of it. Thus Friday cannot be depicted as a complete savage. Crusoe, in fact, becomes dependent on Friday; and it is only with Friday's help that he escapes his island 'imprisonment'. While this can be seen as a foretelling of the colonial situation, it is as well, I believe, an expression of Defoe's dilemma about 'savages'. This is expressed, too, when the 'savages' first land on the island on which Crusoe had been marooned, when he wonders whether 'now was the time to get me a servant, and perhaps a *companion* or an *assistant*' (emphasis mine).[17]

There was also an increase in educational provision – that is, for the upper classes. Many were still educated at home, but some began to attend 'prep' schools: there were twenty-two before 1800.[18] But these, and the 'public' schools already in existence, taught a classical curriculum – all that was necessary for the life of a gentleman, or even for future military and naval commanders. There were also some schools for the middle classes, teaching a similar curriculum; there were none for working-class children. Thus, there was an increasing reading public, and an increasing range of books and publications to cater to it.

The traders and investors in enslaved Africans, who had to justify enslavement, enlarged on the already existing derogation of the Other and began to depict Africans as sub-human in their books. Philosophers, seeking to establish a chain of creation sought a relationship between dark-skinned humans and monkeys. Some, such as David Hume, were adamant that 'negroes [were] naturally inferior to whites'.[19] But, just as the judges continued to disagree about the legality of slavery in England, philosophers could not agree either. For example, in 1752, James Foster wrote that all men were born with a 'natural right to liberty for all mankind are by nature equal'. In 1760, J. Philmore not only agreed about the equality of races, but denied that any race had the 'right to lay commands' on another.[20] When planters claimed that their slaves were intractably lazy, this also found a ready answer. James Beattie in his *Essays on the Nature and Immutability of Truth* (1778) pointed out that it would be unnatural to expect otherwise. A writer in the *London Magazine* of October 1745 commented that a refusal to adapt to slavery and attempts to escape would have been praised had the slaves been Europeans.[21] Defoe came to believe that, before contact with Europeans, 'natives' were 'innocent, humane and moral'.[22]

Malachy Postlethwayt, a writer on economics, bemoaned the existing necessity for the trade in slaves in his *Britain's Commercial Interest*, published in 1757. He suggested the abolition of the trade, the replacement of slave labour with free emigrants, and the exploration of 'the very heart and center of these extensive territories (in Africa). We know little of that infinite variety of vegetable, mineral and animal production . . . which might afford an infinite variety of trafficable objects'. He recognised that this inland trade could not be extended 'to the degree that it is capable of while the spirit of butchery and making slaves of each other is promoted by the Europeans among these people . . . the slaving trade will ever spirit up wars and hostilities among the negro-princes and chiefs, for the sake of making captives of each other for sale'.[23] However, Postlethwayt also proposed that traders should 'fix [themselves] in the favour and friendship of those savage nations'. He also spoke of the need to civilise Africans, but this seems to amount to persuading them of their need for European clothing and furniture, which Britain would happily export to them. Was Postlethwayt, despite his clear understanding of the process of the trade in enslaved Africans, in a quandary similar to that of Defoe, unsure how to understand Africans themselves? Or was he differentiating by class: kings and chiefs and presumably commoners, and those enslaved through warfare?

Historians (a new 'profession') joined the debate, but apparently on one side only. For example, T. Osborne and his co-authors claimed in their *Universal History* (1760) that Africans were 'proud, lazy, treacherous, thievish, hot, and addicted to all kinds of lusts . . . pimps, panders, incestuous, brutish, savage, cruel and revengeful . . . inhuman, drunkards, deceitful, covetous, perfidious'.[24] Perhaps the most influential of these 'historians' was the planter and later justice of the Vice-Admiralty Court in Jamaica, Edward Long, who published his *History of Jamaica* in 1774. Long reiterated all of Osborne's aspersions and added some of his own. Africa was the 'parent of every thing that is monstrous in nature' and the Africans were closer to orang-utans than to Europeans; they were, in fact, a different species. Long, very shrewdly (and factually) argued that the 'trade in slaves and the goods they produced were immensely profitable, not only to the West Indies, but to Britain itself and that it greatly enriched Englishmen in all walks of life'.[25]

Africans and those of African descent were thus homogenised and dehumanised – by some.

One result of this was the experiment conducted by the Duke of Montague regarding the educability (humanity?) of Blacks. Though the sons of African aristocracy as well as the sons of traders on the coast and their African consorts had been sent to acquire English education throughout the century, Montague wanted to settle the issue once and for all. He brought to England from his Jamaican estates Francis Williams, a free Black child. Francis was sent to school and then to the University of Cambridge. A poet and a composer, he lived in the Duke's household before returning to Jamaica in the mid-1730s.[26] Williams was not the only Black who was accepted by some segments of London society. This small Black middle class included Ayuba Suleiman Diallo,[27] George Polgreen Bridgetower,[28] Ignatius Sancho,[29] Julius Soubise[30] and Olaudah Equiano, who moved in radical political circles;[31] also successful entrepreneurs such as Cesar Picton, coal-merchant and freeholder of Kingston, Surrey.[32]

While these elegant, educated Blacks moved in middle-class and even upper-class society, others were being put on the auction block in London, Liverpool and Bristol. Some slaves were appallingly treated, as illustrated by the case of Jonathan Strong, who had been beaten almost to death by his owner (a lawyer and Barbados planter) and thrown on to the London streets as useless in 1765. His experiences with Strong resulted in Granville Sharp's taking many cases on behalf of Black slaves in Britain to court; but none of these succeeded in illegitimising slavery.[33]

Not all slave-servants were treated so brutally. Some managed to obtain wages for their work. Most seemed to work alongside white servants without any problems. Some clearly lived as free men and women: we know of Black churchwardens, crossing sweepers, door-to-door salesmen, seamen, beggars, entertainers and prostitutes. There were many Black participants in the Gordon Riots of 1780, which, while usually depicted as anti-Irish, were in fact against a repressive government and judiciary.[34] That intermarriage was common was noted, for example, by Cobbett, who wrote that 'No black swain need, in this loving country, hang himself in despair . . . if he be not a downright cripple, he will, if he is so disposed, always find a woman'.[35]

That Blacks must have lived next door to whites amicably – that perhaps there was class solidarity – is demonstrated by the fact that Blacks continued to run away from their owners/employers. But where could they run to? There were no swamps as in North America, or mountains as in Jamaica, where they could live as maroons. We must presume that they ran to, and were sheltered by, the mixed working-class communities living in the appalling conditions prevalent in British cities.

Simultaneously with Sharp's series of court cases, John Wesley denounced slavery; the Quakers presented the first anti-slavery petition to Parliament in 1783 and, in 1787, formed the Society for the Abolition of the Slave Trade. The Society organised numerous petitions which were signed by tens of thousands around the country. The logo of the Society became an African breaking his chains, with the inscription, 'Am I not a Man and a Brother?'.

Thus, even at the end of the eighteenth century, there was an ambivalence and a fluidity in perceptions and attitudes towards Black peoples. But the needs of trade and commerce, of incipient empire, began also to have a serious influence on the ideas being propagated. However, it is arguable that these racist notions were still confined to some segments of the reading public, and to some (the majority?) of those who were involved in, or invested in, either the trade in enslaved Africans or in the plantation economies.

The nineteenth and early twentieth centuries

The century began with the revolution in St Domingue and the creation of free, Black-controlled Haiti. This and the French Revolution caused such consternation in Britain that, for a period, the struggle to abolish the trade in slaves was abandoned. It was soon resuscitated and the first of many laws barring all forms of participation in the trade was passed in 1807.[36] An increase in slave revolts and the impossibility of replenishing the slave population (which never reproduced itself in the conditions prevailing in the British 'owned' islands) resulted in the emancipation of slaves in the West Indies.[37]

Britain was thus confronted with the prospect, horrifying to some, of free Blacks – free Blacks unwilling, moreover, to work as wage labour for the pittance offered by their previous owners. How was profit to be made from the plantations, if the labour force was recalcitrant and the price of sugar dropping? How to prove to the British legislature and make publicly acceptable that a new form of unfree labour (indentured) was needed in order to continue making profit?

Another problem was how to replace the lucrative trade in enslaved Africans. As noted previously, it had been advocated by some abolitionists in Britain, even before 1807, that 'legitimate' trade could be profitable. Palm oil was available; so were timber, ivory and some gold. Could cotton be grown? Britons (and other Europeans) began to explore the African hinterlands and river systems to determine what was exploitable.[38] Once these were surveyed and mapped, new trading relationships had to be established and, in some cases, lands, mineral and trading rights acquired against the wishes of the indigenes.[39]

Trading posts on the African coast began to be replaced by colonies which required administrators. The empire began to expand. The imperatives of trade, of attempting to maintain supremacy not only on the seas but in commerce, led to more and more territories being added.[40] In 1858, India was placed under direct British rule.[41] Altogether, some 300 million people were added to the British empire during the century.[42]

There were other new imperatives: a solution had to be found for the burgeoning domestic population which neither the industrial revolution nor the military could absorb. Not only was the population increasing, but it was also becoming politicised: the Chartist movement, for example, demanded universal (male) suffrage and annual parliaments.[43] The Chartists and the growth of trade unionism and socialism were seen as threats to the established order.[44] At first, these unwanted women and men were criminalised and transported, mainly to Australia and Tasmania. When this was deemed inhumane, voluntary emigration was fostered: between 1815 and 1900 about 15 million sailed from the British Isles.[45] No thought was ever given to the displaced indigenous peoples, many of whom were wholly exterminated, others grossly decimated, in this process of 'settlement'.

Expansion, both of empire and industry, required a new coterie of administrators. Expansionist wars required not only officers, but also men who were proud to fight not because their country was attacked, but for the glory of empire. Those forced into or encouraged to emigrate had to be convinced that they had a natural right to the lands they occupied and the working class at home had to be appeased and made proud of its (menial) role in a class-ridden empire. People had to be made to understand that 'an empire such as ours requires as its first condition an imperial race – a race vigorous and industrious and intrepid'.[46] To reinforce these notions, Prime Minister Benjamin Disraeli declared Queen Victoria Empress in 1876. Such ideology could also be put to good use when, towards the end of the century, industrial competition began to threaten Britain's dominance.

Thus there was a conjunction of imperatives: to acquire the empire which was needed as a source of raw materials and purchasers of manufactured products; to provide a viable life for the emigrant poor who were also the future buyers of British goods; to provide an outlet for the adventurous (including traders, planters, etc.) and positions of authority for the new middle classes. And to appease and control an almost rebellious working class. There was a meeting of minds, a recognition, from about mid-century onwards, that these aims could be achieved by revitalising and expanding the Anglo-Saxonism which had been encouraged two hundred years earlier.[47] Moreover, previous versions of racist ideology could now be scientifically justified. All classes could be homogenised into a superior 'English race', while class distinctions within the 'race' were retained. Empire could be justified and glamorised by the duty/necessity of the superior race to export its civilisation to the benighted, racially inferior, heathen hordes.

The writers, philosophers, economists, scientists and politicians, the churches and their missionaries, empire societies, children's and women's organisations for the working class (mostly led by the middle class), the purveyors of popular culture, including magazines and the formal education system, all played their role in producing this new national ideology of beneficent imperialism, of English superiority and of national unity.[48]

A brief glimpse at these agencies of indoctrination will have to suffice.[49]

The politicians and empire-builders
These are the men who held sway, who caught the public imagination, who set the tone of discourse, whose attitudes were emulated. A very brief selection of quotes is sufficient to indicate their attitudes:

Cecil Rhodes, 1895: 'in order to save the 40 million inhabitants of the UK from a bloody civil war, we colonial statesmen must acquire new lands to settle the surplus population, to provide new markets for the goods produced by them . . . If you want to avoid civil war you must become imperialists.'[50]

Joseph Chamberlain, 1896: 'Local government . . . is the curse of the West Indies. In many islands it means only the rule of a local oligarchy of whites and half-breeds . . . In other cases it is the rule of the Negroes – totally unfit for representative institutions.'[51]

Earl Grey, 1896 (on the death of Hubert Hervey in the second Matabele war): 'It is a grand thing to die for the expansion of Empire . . . He sacrificed [himself] for duty . . . the type of Englishman [who] made the British Empire what it is today.'[52]

Joseph Chamberlain, 1900: 'I believe in this race, the greatest governing race, so proud, self-confident and determined, this race, which neither climate nor change can degenerate, which will infallibly be the predominant force of future history and universal civilisation.'[53]

Lord Milner, 1901 (in a despatch to Chamberlain): 'I do not mean that they [Africans] should be educated like Europeans, for their requirements and capacities are very different . . .Undoubtedly the greatest benefit that could be bestowed upon them would be to teach them habits of regular and skilled labour.'[54]

Lord Milner, 1912: 'It is we who have been foremost in opening up the great waste spaces of the New World, and filling them with peoples of a high standard of civilisation. It is we who have brought peace and justice, and given orderly and humane government, to hundreds of millions of the weaker or more backward races These new lands of immense promise inhabited by men of our race, these ancient lands restored to order and civilisation by our agency, are the two great moral assets of Imperialism.'[55]

Sir Harry Johnston, 1920: 'On the continent of Africa we have little but backward peoples to deal with . . . There is sufficient white blood in the Abyssinian to let one hope they may some day of their own free will enter the fold of civilized peoples . . . The chief and obvious distinction between backward and forward peoples is that the former . . . are of coloured skin . . . Obviously the foremost nations of the world are the British and the regions of the British Empire in which the white race predominates.'[56]

General Sir Ian Hamilton, 1936 (on the death of Rudyard Kipling): 'His death seems to me to place a full stop to the period when war was a romance and the expansion of the Empire a duty.'[57]

Sir Fiennes Cecil Arthur Barrett-Lennard, retired Chief Justice of Jamaica, 1934: 'Cruelty is a characteristic of the Negro . . . Contacts between Africans and Europeans often result in infecting the higher race with one or more of the vices of the inferior race.'[58]

Formal education
Free, compulsory education for *all* children up to the age of 10 was not established till 1880 when basic literacy and numeracy became necessary for the efficient functioning of an industrialised and expansionist society. (The curriculum included military drill.) Until then, working-class children could attend the Sunday and day schools provided by the churches, which taught religion and the 'three Rs'. Schools for the middle class vastly increased in number.[59]

Britain's 'public' schools from the mid-Victorian era were suffused with rituals and were designed to create notions of English and, of course, class superiority towards a hierarchy of others.[60] It was recognised that pomp and circumstance – public and private rituals – were all important in enshrining and promulgating power and status. Athleticism – playing the game – was at the core of public school education and was then exported to the state schools.[61]

As taught in all these schools, imperialism became the almost divine mission of particular *races*, most especially the English. (The French and Germans held similar notions.) It was the English alone who had the strength, courage, discipline and self-sacrifice to go on civilising missions to the dark corners of the ever-growing empire; fighting and dying for 'your nation' was preferable to staying 'mouldily alive in some ignoble commercial and materialist way of life'.[62] As recalled by Robert Roberts in his *Classic Slum,* 'teachers, fed on Seeley's *The Expansion of the English,* spelled out patriotism among us with a fervour that with some edged on the religious'.[63]

The typical Englishman, as propagated by the textbooks eventually used in all schools, was an honest, industrious Anglo-Saxon, loyal to the team, brave, calm and courageous in the face of danger.[64] This racial/national superiority was dependent on 'the creation of the imperial subject [on whom] are built the deepest hopes and fears of the imperialist nations . . . Securing the youth into the imperial ethos involved both positive identification with Britishness and distancing from the undesirable Other.'[65] History and geography texts all propagated such notions.[66]

How was the Other depicted in the texts?[67] The notions of racial hierarchy which were the bedrock of social Darwinism and the eugenics movement are clearly evident in the texts of the late nineteenth century, most of which were in use for decades. The colonies and India are presented as having had no history prior to the arrival of Europeans; subject peoples welcome their British conquerors. Stereotyping abounds. For example, Indians and Afghans are invariably cruel (there is much emphasis on 'Oriental cruelty') and savage, while their leaders are despotic, weak, effeminate and treacherous, and unfitted to rule themselves.[68]

To take just a few examples: in *England in the Nineteenth Century* (1899), Sir Charles Oman taught pupils that 'emancipated slaves were idle and disorderly; when the fear of the lash was removed, they did not take kindly to work . . . The Aborigines of Australia . . . were among the lowest and most barbarous of mankind.' 'Foreigners' were invariably described by Sir Charles as 'reckless', 'fanatical', 'unbalanced', 'frantic', 'treacherous' and 'malicious'.[69] In a crib to accompany his textbook, *New History of England and Great Britain* (1895), John Meiklejohn, Professor of Education at St Andrews University, stated, for example:

1856: Annexation of Oudh. Oudh was a rich country in the North of India – annexed by Lord Dalhousie in consequence of the cruelties and misgovernment of the sovereign . . . 1860: The Convention of Pekin. The allied armies of England and France entered Pekin; and the Emperor agreed to all they wanted.[70]

Yet another text, Rudyard Kipling's and C. R. L. Fletcher's *A School History of England*, first published in 1911 and still in use in the 1950s, described West Indians as 'lazy, vicious, incapable of serious improvement, or of work except under compulsion'.

The headmasters of public schools expounded similar ideologies. Frederic Farrar, headmaster at Marlborough, espoused racial theories, including the hierarchy of races.[71] Headmaster Weller of Harrow stated in 1895 that education must relate to the administration of the empire; the purpose of public schools must be the production of generals, governors and statesmen, whose 'role arose out of the colonising genius of the English – the product of racial superiority'. It was to sports at the public schools, Weller maintained, that England owed its sovereignty.[72]

University lecturers, as noted above, held similar views.[73] John Ruskin, Slade Professor of Fine Art at Oxford, in his 1870 inaugural lecture spoke of the 'destiny now before us . . . We are still undegenerate in race . . . [England] must found colonies as fast and as far as she is able . . . seizing every piece of fruitful waste ground.'[74] Sir John Seeley, Regius Professor of Modern History at the University of Cambridge, believed in the importance of inheritance, that is, of 'blood'. 'The Spanish Empire', he wrote in 1894, 'had the fundamental defect of not being European in blood. Not only did the part of the population which was European belong to a race which even in Europe was in decline, but there was another large part which had a mixture of barbarism in its blood, and another larger still, whose blood was purely barbaric.'[75] While arguing that 'our colonies were in the main planted in the emptier parts of the globe', Seeley admitted that India was populous. But 'a most deplorable anarchy reigned there', before the British arrived to create order.[76] James Froude, who held the equivalent professorship at Oxford, visited the West Indies in 1887 and opined that 'negro women's grace of body cannot compensate for their colour, which now that they are free is harder to bear than when they were slaves'. West Indians of African descent were of an 'inferior race', which could only ever hope to reach 'the white man's level' if led by whites. 'Conscious of their native inferiority, [they] are docile and willing to work if anyone will direct them', Froude wrote. Africans themselves were 'savage within their natural state . . . would domesticate like sheep and oxen'.[77]

Informal education: philosophers and scientists[78]
Charles Darwin's *Origin of the Species* was published in 1859 and

developed the theory of the survival of the fittest. It was but a simple step for his interpreters to argue that the speedy decline of native populations after the arrival of the Europeans was due to such a process of 'natural selection': only the 'fittest' nations would survive.[79] Social Darwinism and eugenicist philosophies during that period went hand in hand with the creation of stereotypes: superior for the British and inferior for just about everybody else.[80] Books such as Lord Avebury's *The Origin of Civilisation and the Primitive Condition of Man: mental and social condition of savages* were highly popular. Originating as a series of lectures at the Royal Institution in 1868, it was in its sixth edition by 1902. Avebury, who was an officer or member of dozens of learned societies in Britain, Europe and the US, had been in discussion with others of his ilk regarding the finer points of his book, which begins by claiming that:

> the lower races of men . . . present us with illustrations of a social condition ruder, more archaic than any which . . . ever existed among the more advanced races . . . The stronger and progressive increase in numbers and drive out the weaker and lower races.

Richard Drayton has demonstrated in his book *Nature's Government* how the new sciences were used to make conquest seem necessary, legitimate and beneficial.[81]

Learned and imperial societies
A whole host of societies, some 'learned', were established to educate the middle classes and promulgate the latest scientific and political notions. One such was the Colonial Society, formed in 1869. Its aims, according to old Etonian William Gladstone, included 'handing down from generation to generation the great and noble tradition of the unity of the British *race*' (emphasis mine).[82] Another was the Royal Anthropological Society, founded in 1863. Its founder and chairman, James Hunt, was a follower of the Scottish anatomist Robert Knox, who believed that the 'dark races' were physically and mentally inferior to whites. Hunt was a firm believer in racial hierarchies, and also espoused eugenicist notions of racial degeneracy.[83] H. W. Wyatt, a founder of the Imperial Maritime League, believed that 'savages . . . had little claim to the vast living space they inhabited' and hence Europeans, especially the British, had every right to appropriate their lands.[84] A society with a slightly different interest was the Imperial Institute, founded in 1886–8 under the aegis of the Prince of Wales. It served as a meeting place for imperialists and sponsored exhibitions, lectures, conferences and 'scientific and technological work to assist the expansion of trade and the exploration and utilisation of natural resources' within the empire. The empire was thus seen and promoted in purely utilitarian terms. Ethical questions,

such as by what right Britain explored and exploited, were never discussed or, probably, even conceived.

Other organisations recognised the necessity of spreading the imperialist message to the lower classes who did not attend Imperial Institute lectures.[85] One such was the Primrose League, founded in 1883, whose aim was the 'maintenance of the imperial ascendance of the British Empire'. It produced children's fiction and leaflets; mounted exhibitions; held lectures and magic lantern shows to demonstrate that the British civilising mission would eventually lift the 'natives' from their barbarism. The League propagated the ideology of the Christian military hero. Another organisation aimed at working-class people and their children was the Empire Day Movement, founded by the Earl of Meath in 1892, which promoted the celebration of Empire Day throughout the empire.[86] An example of its ideology can be found in Mary Debenham's *Empire Day: a dialogue for children*. Children taking the roles of the colonies in this 'dialogue' all address Britannia as 'Mother'. In reply to the question 'who is Britannia?', a boy replies, 'She's on the pennies, with a good sharp spear/ To prog the folks who dare to interfere/"Hands off"', she says, "from what belongs to me/ I rule the waves and always shall, you'll see."' Another boy says: 'Empire Day is meant for people who can fight; soldiers and sailors . . . It's kept to remind us how we've always won.' The children representing Africa and the West Indies only have two lines to say in greeting Britannia, while the others have eight.[87]

Children's organisations
The Boys' Brigade was formed in 1883 in Glasgow to teach 'Christian manliness to street-corner boys'; by 1890 it had 16,000 members, mainly from the 'respectable' working class, being inculcated with notions of patriotism, loyalty and duty to the flag.[88] Other youth movements with similar aims were the Salvation and the Church armies, which pursued and embellished the notion of the Christian military hero, fighting the evils of savagery and barbarism among the heathen who had to be saved (and subjugated) for Christ. The scouting movement, which held its first camp in 1907, was started by Robert Baden-Powell; he stated that its 'over-riding concern [was] imperial defence and *racial* survival' (emphasis mine).[89] Naturally he believed that the Darwinian idea of the survival of the fittest applied to nations as well as people.

Missionaries
Missionaries were not only primary agents of cultural imperialism, but also opened the way for the traders and settlers who followed in their wake.[90] Livingstone is a prime example of the missionary who regarded Africans as children and savages. His aim was to 'open Africa to

commerce and Christianity . . . [he] seemed to his successors to have provided the moral basis for massive imperialist expansion'. Livingstone's *Missionary Travels* sold 70,000 copies; Stanley's *In Darkest Africa,* 150,000.[91]

There were other agencies of racial indoctrination. In order to raise funds, the missionaries had to promulgate the notion of the misbegotten heathen who was in dire need of saving from the fires of hell. For example, in a book for children, M. A. S. Barber describes nearly all natives as cannibals and idolators, fates from which the brave missionaries will save them. The missionaries also display much fortitude in the inhospitable climates where most of these natives seem to live; they even venture out to Barbados and Jamaica to 'teach the poor negroes'.[92]

Children's and adult literature
G. A. Henty and Rudyard Kipling were the primary producers of imperialist tales for the young; Kipling's creed was described by the French historian Elie Halévy as a 'species of Darwinian philosophy expressed in a mythical form . . . a moral code, chaste, brutal, heroic and childlike'.[93] Among others inculcating such notions were R. M. Ballantyne, Edgar Rice Burroughs and Captain Marryat (whose scurrilous works are currently being republished).

There were many books of heroism written for children and young people. One author described his work as 'written not to glorify war but to nourish patriotism'. His *Deeds That Won the Empire*, said W. H. Fitchett, were 'tales of fortitude: of loyalty to duty stronger than the love of life . . . of patriotism which makes love of the Fatherland a passion . . . These are the elements of a robust citizenship.'[94]

From the late Victorian period, there was a massive expansion of boys' periodicals, propagating nationalism ('the master nation/race'), racial stereotyping and class attitudes. *The Boy's Own Paper* held a conference where it was decided that 'True imperialism' meant the 'salvation of heathens'. Howard Spicer, the editor of the most jingoistic of these publications, *The Boy's Own Empire*, went on to found the Boys' Empire League.[95]

During this period, the 'public appetite for exciting, patriotic adventure and interest in the customs of exotic aliens' grew apace.[96] Among the hundreds of books which aimed to fulfil the desire for the latter, Dudley Kidd's *The Essential Kaffir* can be used as an example of the genre. He presented a composite, homogenised picture of Africans in South Africa, who were

> incapable of developing mentally beyond a certain stage . . . [they] have made but little progress during the last few centuries . . . hopelessly lazy . . . thriftless, improvident . . . They have no ambitions . . .

have no grit or balance . . . The school Kaffir is frequently a very objectionable person . . . The natives must be more or less the drudges of the white men, owing to their inherent inferiority and incapacity.[97]

The heroes of many novels were bent on taming the wilderness; on bringing order to the chaos of savage life; on bringing the benefits of British culture, of civilisation and Christianity, to the darkness prevailing in much of the empire; and on confirming the superiority of being English. Among such novelists were Rider Haggard, Rudyard Kipling, John Buchan, William Thackeray and Conan Doyle.[98]

The press
The uprising in India in 1857 (denigrated by the British as a 'mutiny') occasioned what was probably the first great outpouring of racism in the British press. Though there was no evidence of the rape of English women, the ubiquitous implication was that they had been. In the words of historian Denis Judd:

> the Victorian public was gorged on the horrors of the uprising. Cartoons and drawings in newspapers and journals expressed a predictable sense of national outrage while at the same time titillating their readers' imaginations with lurid, and generally irresponsible, images of mayhem. Indian troops were shown tossing British babies on their bayonets for sport . . . A print depicted a pair of dishevelled and bloodstained mutineers about to lay their reeking hands upon the heads of defenceless infants and upon the bosom of a breast-feeding British mother . . .The most telling of the [outraged responses] was a sense of betrayal . . . The [Indians] who rose in rebellion . . .were all denounced as ungrateful and treacherous wretches, unmindful of the benefits bestowed by Britain's civilising mission.[99]

The late nineteenth century also saw the publication of 'penny dreadfuls' and the *Penny Magazine*, all replete with the power of the white man and the inferiority of all other races; the savagery of the Black, the inscrutability and wiliness of the Oriental and the effeminacy of the Indian, who was fit at best to be the servant of the Englishman. These themes were repeated on postcards and advertisements; in the new newspapers such as the *National Observer* (1888–1893) and *Daily Mail* (1896–);[100] in the illustrations in magazines such as the *Illustrated London News*, the *Graphic* and the *Pall Mall Gazette*; on the walls of art galleries and in the pages of works of travel and of fiction, for both adults and juveniles.[101]

Popular culture.

Popular exhibitions to educate (or indoctrinate) the public began with the Great Exhibition of 1851, which included only about sixty exhibits on empire. It was followed by the Colonial and Indian Exhibition of 1886. These empire exhibitions were held regularly until after the second world war.[102] Millions attended to learn about the success of the civilising mission and to view 'natives' in tableaux of village life, given such titles as 'Savage South Africa' and the 'Kaffir Kraal'. The public was also entertained by theatrical spectacles of 'The Kaffir War', 'Zulu Chief', 'Cetawayo at Last' and, adding a little sexual thrill to imperialism, 'The Geisha' and 'Chinese Honeymoon'. These all extolled the invincibility of British might and 'civilised' methods of warfare, in contrast with 'native' savagery and brutality. According to John MacKenzie, there was another aspect to the symbolism: yesterday's barbaric foe, conquered by British strength and courage, was so subjugated that today he could be – and was content to be – an exhibit.[103]

Magic lantern shows and, later, photography also played a role in purveying negative, and sometimes highly sexualised, images of the Other. In the words of historian Brian Street, 'for the general public at the turn of the century, images of other societies with their underlying associations of race, hierarchy and evolution, were most vividly expressed through exhibitions, photographs and postcards'.[104] The ubiquitous Lord Meath was on the Committee of the Board of Education's Visual Instruction Committee.[105]

All these shows and the hugely popular music hall performances served to introduce or reinforce racial stereotypes and establish a racial hierarchy in the popular mind. The necessity of fighting to defend/expand empire and the sense of national superiority were reinforced by such songs as 'we don't want to fight, but, by jingo if we do/ we've got the ships, we've got the men, we've got the money too'.[106]

Then there were the soldiers returning from duty in the empire, who had been well indoctrinated with the appropriate attitudes to take towards the 'fuzzy-wuzzies' or the 'effeminate' Indians.[107]

After the first world war

Given such a level of indoctrination, it is to be expected that the population would have become prejudiced towards Black peoples. The results of the first survey to determine this were published in 1928. The researcher asked 315 people two simple questions: would you let a coloured person come to your home? and would you let your children associate with those of good coloured people? Forty-seven were doubtful – but 254 gave an unequivocal 'No'. Of twenty hotels questioned, only two said that they would admit 'African or Indian natives as guests'.[108] Two years later, research with schoolchildren showed that 'prejudice exists in children throughout the whole school life'.[109]

The first recorded lynching of a Black man (witnessed by the police who did not intervene) took place in 1919, by which time verbal and physical attacks on Black peoples in British streets were not uncommon.[110] There were anti-Black riots in many cities. The government took action by restricting employment opportunities for Black seamen. Though the new law was meant to apply only to 'Coloured *Alien* seamen', the Home Office instruction stated that it was to apply to *all* coloured men.[111]

With the 1930s came a resurgence of eugenicism. The Eugenics Society, whose members included Keynes, Julian Huxley and the director of the London School of Economics, pressed for voluntary sterilisation of 'mental defectives'.[112] Working-class children were held to be innately inferior. At least one member of the society advocated the prevention of the 'intermixture of white and coloured races', as 'race mixture' led to the mongrelisation of offspring.[113] These 'half-caste' children were deemed to be a problem (mainly because they couldn't find employment) and were stated to be less intelligent than white children.[114] In 1931, *The Spectator*, as well as printing a series of highly racist articles, noted the growing racial prejudice in England.[115] In 1940, the Colonial Office's Welfare Officer commented that 'colour prejudice in the United Kingdom is widespread'.[116]

Education continued to play its role. Herbert Gray had complained in 1913 that there was little 'interest and instruction' regarding overseas dominions and advocated a 'system of physical, moral and mental training [that] would free adolescents from all suspicion of insular prejudices'.[117] In 1927, the president of the Board of Education stated that 'it ought to be perfectly clearly laid down by the Board of Education that patriotism is the very foundation of our teaching in schools'.[118] Responding to a complaint by the visiting education officer from Uganda that schoolchildren did not know where the colony was, in 1939, the Colonial Office discovered that 'there was little teaching and no satisfactory texts' on the British colonies. The League of Coloured People examined twenty-four secondary texts and six elementary texts and found 'the subject of Coloured Peoples virtually disregarded in the History books', while those that did contain anything repeated clearly not outworn prejudices.[119]

In 1944 came the publication of Julian Huxley's and Phyllis Deane's *The Future of the Colonies,* eighth in the popular *Target for Tomorrow* series.[120] This 'liberal' publication acknowledged no responsibility, no instrumentality, in producing the deplorable state of the colonies which it described. 'The poverty of the native reflects the poverty of his country', Huxley opined, clearly not expecting anyone to question the reasons for the European presence in these apparent countries of 'poverty'. 'His ignorance and his political backwardness arise out of its natural poverty . . . It will require European ingenuity to wrest from tropical Africa a real income . . . How are the primitive people of the colonies to be equipped to deal with the crippling problems of drought, disease, hurricanes, soil poverty, ignorance and social disintegration?' Huxley is so 'backward' himself that, in a publication with numbers of portraits of Africans, not one has been named.

Given this milieu, it is not surprising that, in 1949, the *Royal Commission on Population* (Cmd 7695) recommended that emigration from the UK should continue, as a drop in numbers would be of serious consequence 'for Britain's economic future and her place in the world'. The shortfall in labour could be made up from immigrants who '*were of good human stock and were not prevented by their religion or race from intermarrying with the host population and becoming merged in it*' (paras. 329, 331; emphasis mine). This eugenicist recommendation was overtaken by events: Britain had to recruit labour from the colonies and India, which led to large-scale voluntary migration, stopped by legislation from 1962 onwards.

Empire in the nineteenth century sense is long gone. What we are left with is racism, personal and institutional. Research indicates that racism is embedded in all the institutions of our society. The education system and the books in use in schools have not improved. I doubt that more schoolchildren today would know where to find Uganda on a world map than knew sixty-odd years ago.[121] All too little has been done by the government to overcome the racism engendered in the previous one hundred years. Furthermore, the new imperialism, whether perpetrated by the IMF, the World Bank, the multinationals, western governments or sex tourists, continues to be based on notions of white (racial) superiority.

References

1 See, e.g., Dorothea Matlitzki, *The Matter of Araby in Medieval England* (New Haven, CT, Yale University Press, 1977); David C. Linberg (ed.), *Science in the Middle Ages* (Chicago, IL, Chicago University Press, 1978).

2 Peter Fryer, *Staying Power* (London, Pluto Press, 1984), pp. 2–5; on Luce Morgan, see, e.g., Hugh Clavert, *Shakespeare's Sonnets* (Devon, Merlin Books, 1987).

3 For example, the Earl of Leicester apparently paid his Black servant/s handsomely (Simon Adams, 'At home and away: the Earl of Leicester', *History Today* (May 1996), pp. 22–28, and subsequent correspondence with the author). There are six 'negroes' or 'blackamores' listed in the *Assessment of Strangers* in the London borough of Barking's All Hallow parish for the years 1598–1599: they are noted, for example, as 'a negra at Olyver Skinnar's'. Status is not recorded. (*Notes & Queries* (April 1961), p. 138.)

4 Published in 1586, the poem reads: 'Leave off with pain, the blackamoor to scour/

With washing oft, and wiping more than due/For thou shalt find, that Nature of power/Do what thou canst, to keep his former hue.'

5 Winthrop D Jordan, *White over Black* (New York, W. W. Norton, 1968), p. 15.

6 D. Hammond and A. Jablow, *The Africa That Never Was* (New York, Twayne, 1970), p. 20.

7 See, for example, Katherine George, 'The civilized West looks at primitive Africa: 1400–1800, *Isis* (1958), pp. 49, 62–72. Parish records from the late sixteenth century use 'black', 'negro', 'nigra', and 'blackamore' as descriptive terms for people of various origins.

8 I have been unable to discover whether Lok entered the 'nefarious trade'.

9 Paul Hair, 'Attitudes to Africans in English primary sources on Guinea up to 1650', *History in Africa* (No. 26, 1999).

10 Another example is Muly Mahomet, the evil hero in Thomas Peele's *The Battle of Alcazar, c.*1588.

11 Quoted in Ruth Cowling, 'Blacks in English renaissance drama', in David Dabydeen (ed.), *The Black Presence in English Literature* (Manchester, Manchester University Press, 1985), p. 4. See also Eldred Jones, *Othello's Countrymen* (Oxford, OUP, 1965); Ania Loomba, *Gender, Race and Renaissance Drama* (Manchester, Manchester University Press, 1989); Anthony G. Barthelemy, *Black Face, Maligned Race* (Baton Rouge, Louisiana State University Press, 1987).

12 The most recent and comprehensive book on slave traders is Hugh Thomas, *The Slave Trade* (London, Picador, 1997). For the pre-Atlantic slave trade, see W. D. Phillips, *Slavery from Roman Times* (Manchester, Manchester University Press, 1985).

13 Folarin Shyllon, *Black People in Britain 1555–1833* (London, OUP, 1977), pp. 17–19.

14 See Hugh A. MacDougall, *Racial Myth in English History* (Montreal, Harvest House, 1982). On how Europe has invented and re-invented itself, see the far-ranging *The Distorted Past: a re-interpretation of Europe*, by Joseph Fontana (Oxford, Blackwell, 1995).

15 Henry Morley (ed.), *The Earlier Life and the Chief Earliest Works of Daniel Defoe* (London, George Routledge, 1889), pp. 189–90. While not specifically naming Africans, could one argue that Defoe was aware of Africans among the Roman auxiliaries stationed in Britain?

16 A most informative book on how earlier improvements helped Europeans' ventures is Carlo M. Cipolla, *Guns, Sails and Empires: technological innovation 1400–1700*, (London, Minerva Press, 1965).

17 Daniel Defoe, *Robinson Crusoe* (1719) (London, J. M. Dent, 1945), p. 147. There were three editions of the book in the year it was published; it is still read today.

18 Donald Leinster-Mackay, *The Rise of the English Prep School* (Lewes, Falmer Press, 1984), p. 16.

19 David Hume, in an essay entitled 'Of national character' (1753), quoted in Fryer, op. cit., n. 2, p. 152.

20 James Foster, *Discourses on all the Principal Branches of Natural Religion and Social Virtues* (London, 1752) and J. Philmore, *Two Dialogues of the Man-Trade* (London, 1760), quoted in Julia M. Reed, 'The origins of English attitudes towards the Black Africans 1554–1807', MA Thesis, University of Hull, 1975, pp. 172 et seq.

21 Reed, ibid.

22 Defoe's *In Madagascar* (1729), quoted in Martin Green, *Dreams of Adventure, Deeds of Empire* (London, Routledge and Kegan Paul, 1980), p. 362.

23 Postlethwayt (1707?–1767) was elected as fellow of the Society of Arts in 1734; a prolific author, his publications include a number on the African slave trade, which broadly repeat the above argument and advocate that the East India

Company, whatever its faults, should take over and expand trade with Africa. Quotations from volume 2, pp. 215 and 268–9.

24 Fryer, op. cit., n. 2, p. 153.

25 Ibid., pp. 159–60. Long, the son of a plantation owner, had also been private secretary to the lieutenant governor of Jamaica, Sir Henry Moore. He married the sole heiress of Thomas Beckford, Jamaican planter/merchant.

26 Despite the Duke's patronage, Williams was refused government employment on his return to Jamaica. On Williams and other 'middle-class' Africans in Britain, see Fryer, op. cit., n. 2; Shyllon, op. cit., n. 13; E. Scobie, *Black Britannia* (Chicago, IL, Johnson Publishing, 1972); James Walvin, *Black and White* (London, Allen Lane, 1973).

27 Diallo was the enslaved son of a Fula priest. On learning of the slave's scholarship (he wrote fluent Arabic), the Royal African Society purchased his freedom and brought him to London where he was elected member of a very prestigious antiquarian society. After helping Sir Hans Sloane with some Arabic translations, the much-feted young man was shipped home to Africa. See Douglas Grant, *The Fortunate Slave* (London, OUP, 1968).

28 Recognised as a child prodigy, Bridgetower became the Prince of Wales's first violinist and performed in many British and European cities.

29 Another Montague protégé, Ignatius Sancho became a Mayfair grocer and composer who moved in London's artistic circles; his *Letters of the Late Ignatius Sancho* was published in 1782. See also Reyahn King et al (eds), *Ignatius Sancho: an African man of Letters* (London, National Portrait Gallery, 1997) and P. Edwards and P. Rewt, *The Letters of Ignatius Sancho* (Edinburgh, Edinburgh University Press, 1994).

30 Julius Soubise of St Kitts was educated as a gentleman by the Duchess of Queensberry; handsome, polished, a violinist, orator, swordsman and equestrian, he apparently moved freely in aristocratic salons.

31 Olaudah Equiano, an enslaved Ibo who had purchased his own freedom, became a government employee for a while in England, and was part of the abolitionist movement, lecturing around Britain and Ireland. His book, *The Interesting Narrative of the Life of Olaudah Equiano*, published in 1789, went through nine British editions in his lifetime; it was also published in New York and was translated into Dutch, German and Russian. The most recent edition of Equiano's work, edited by Vincent Carretta, was published by Penguin in 1995. See also James Walvin, *An African's Life: the life and times of Olaudah Equiano 1745–1797* (London, Cassell, 1998).

32 See Black & Asian Studies Association *Newsletter* (No. 27, April 2000).

33 Granville Sharp and the indefatigable Thomas Clarkson were the two pre-eminent workers for abolition in Britain. There is no modern biography of Sharp, but see Prince Hoare, *Memoirs of Granville Sharp* (London, 1828). On Clarkson, see Ellen Gibson Wilson, *Thomas Clarkson: a biography* (Basingstoke, Macmillan Press, 1989).

34 See Marika Sherwood, 'Blacks in the Gordon Riots', *History Today* (December 1997), pp. 24–8.

35 Reid, op. cit., n. 20, p. 142. Cobbett did not approve, describing intermarriage as 'foul, unnatural and detestable'. (*Weekly Political Review* (16 June 1804), pp. 935–7.) James Tobin in 1785 had written that 'the strange partiality shewn for [blacks] by the lower order of women, the rapid increase of a dark and contaminated breed, are evils'. (James Tobin, *Cursory Remarks upon the Reverend Mr Ramsey's Essay*, London, 1785, quoted in Shyllon, op. cit., n. 13, p. 104.)

36 One of the latest books on abolition is Robin Blackburn, *The Overthrow of Colonial Slavery* (London, Verso, 1988). There were many ways of contravening the laws; see Marika Sherwood, 'Perfidious Albion: Britain, the USA, and slavery in the

1840s and 1860s', *Contributions to Black Studies* (Nos 13/14, 1998/1999) and 'Oh what a tangled web we weave: Britain, the slave trade and slavery 1808–1840', *African Labour* (No. 1, 2000).

37 There is some ongoing discussion regarding deliberate attempts at 'slave-breeding' in Barbuda and Tobago. See Stanley Engerman and B. W. Higman, 'The demographic structure of Caribbean slave society in the 18th and 19th centuries', in Franklin W. Knight (ed.), *General History of the Caribbean, volume 3* (UNESCO, 1997). Debate on the reasons for abolition and emancipation, begun by Eric Williams's *Slavery and Capitalism* (1944) (London, Andre Deutsch, 1965), continues to this day. The freed men, women and children received no compensation but their ex-owners were paid £20m in compensation for their loss of free labour. Much of this was invested in Britain. (Anthony Wood, *Nineteenth Century Britain* (New York, David Mackay, 1962), p. 206.) For an interesting aspect of the abolitionist movement, see Clare Midgley, *Women Against Slavery* (London, Routledge, 1992).

38 On the British relationship with Africa, see, e.g., R. Robinson and J. Gallagher, *Africa and the Victorians* (New York, St Martin's Press, 1961); H. L. Wesseling, *Divide and Rule* (Westport, CT, Praeger, 1996).

39 On these early explorations and settlements, see, e.g., Christopher Lloyd, *The Search for the Niger* (Newton Abbott, Readers' Union, 1973); Howard J. Pedraza, *Borrioboola-Gha* (London, OUP, 1960) and Obaro Ikeme, *The Fall of Nigeria* (London, Heinemann, 1977).

40 The Cape Colony began to be settled in 1815; King Cetewayo of the Zulus was defeated in 1879; soon after Uganda was made a British Protectorate, as was 'Rhodesia' and the Sudan was conquered. To prevent further fights with each other for territory, the European powers divided up Africa between themselves at the Berlin Conference of 1885. At the turn of the century, the defeat of the Boers led to their territories being added to British South Africa; in 1902, the Ashanti were conquered. In the East, Hong Kong had been ceded to Britain in 1840 and Kowloon had been leased from China in 1860. For the view from 'the other side', see A. Adu Boahen, *African Perspectives on Colonialism* (Baltimore, MD, Johns Hopkins University Press, 1987). An interesting exposition on expansion, rivalry and conquest can be found in Giles Merton, *Nathaniel's Nutmeg* (London, Hodder, 1999).

41 India's neighbours were conquered by the British-officered Indian armies; both the British officers and the army were paid out of Indian revenues. On this expansion, see the interestingly titled chapter, 'Imperial defence 1870–1897', *Cambridge History of the British Empire* (Cambridge, CUP, 1959).

42 The historian J. R. Seeley, in a fit of his own absent-mindedness, wrote in his *Expansion of England* (1883) that 'we seem, as it were, to have conquered and peopled half the world in a fit of absence of mind'. Quoted in L. C. B. Seaman, *Victorian England*, (London, Methuen, 1973), p. 332. For another view on the acquisition of empire, see Sven Lindquist, *'Exterminate the Brutes'* (London, Granta, 1992). I must thank my friend and colleague Martin Spafford for bringing this book to my attention.

43 The population increased from 26.7 million in 1841 to 41.5 million in 1901.

44 There were Blacks in the Chartist movement, even in leadership positions; thus, in mid-century there still could not have been pervasive racial antagonism, at least within the politicised working class.

45 See W. A. Carrothers, *Emigration from the British Isles* (1929) (London, Frank Cass, 1965), pp. 305–6. Some of these migrants were assisted by private ('philanthropic') emigration societies, others received assistance from the state. For example, some 630,000 were helped to emigrate to Australia between 1832 and 1900. (Ibid., p. 317.) See also, e.g., C. F. Plant, *Overseas Settlement* (London,

OUP, 1951); Alex G. Scholes, *Education for Empire Settlement* (London, Longmans Green, 1932). Children and women were sometimes forcibly made to emigrate. See, e.g., Joan Foster, 'Children from Newcastle', *Local History Magazine* (No. 59, 1997), pp. 14–17; Gillian Wagner, *Children of the Empire* (London, Weidenfeld & Nicolson, 1982); P. Bean and J. Melville, *Lost Children of the Empire* (London, Unwin Hyman, 1989). The only working-class emigration society appears to have been the Potters' Joint Stock Emigration Society and Savings Fund, formed in 1844, which bought land in the US on which 384 families settled. (J. Ginswick, *Labour and the Poor in England and Wales 1849–1851: volume II* (London, Frank Cass, 1983), p. 129.)

46 Lord Rosebery, a Privy Councillor, speaking in 1900, quoted in H. John Field, *Toward a Programme of Imperial Life* (Westport, CT, Greenwood Press, 1982), p. 91.

47 See, e.g., Stuart Anderson, *Race and Rapprochement: Anglo-Saxonism and Anglo-American relations 1895–1904* (Rutherford, Fairleigh-Dickinson University Press, 1981) and Louis L. Snyder, *The Idea of Racialism* (Princeton, D. van Nostrand, 1962).

48 Did Gladstone believe that the indoctrination over empire had, by 1878, been successful when he declared that 'the sentiment of empire may be called innate in every Briton'? (Seaman, op. cit., n. 42, p. 331.)

49 There were – and are – no agencies which systematically counter these ideologies. For an interesting compilation of quotations, see Philip D. Curtin (ed.), *Imperialism* (New York, Harper & Row, 1971).

50 Rhodes quoted in Green, op. cit., n. 22, p. 399, n. 17.

51 Joseph Chamberlain, Secretary of State for the Colonies (and the father of the future Secretary of State for India, Austen) quoted in H. A. Will, *Constitutional Change in the British West Indies* (Oxford, Clarendon Press, 1970), p. 232. On Chamberlain, see, e.g., W. L. Strauss, *Joseph Chamberlain and the Theory of Imperialism* (New York, Fertig, 1971).

52 Foreign Secretary Grey, quoted in Field, op. cit., n. 46, p. 84.

53 V. E. Chancellor, *History for Their Masters* (Bath, Adams & Dart, 1970), p. 115.

54 C. Headlam (ed.), *The Milner Papers: volume II* (London, Cassell, 1933), p. 307.

55 Lord Milner, *The Nation and the Empire* (London, Constable, 1913), p. 490.

56 Sir Harry Johnston, *The Backward Peoples and our Relations with them* (Oxford, OUP, 1920), pp. 23, 26, 7, 9. Johnston, explorer and empire builder, served as, e.g., British Commissioner for South Central Africa 1891–6 and Special Commissioner, Uganda, 1899–1901.

57 Martin Green, *Dreams of Adventure, Deeds of Empire* (London, Routledge and Kegan Paul, 1980), p. 283. Kipling was a close friend of Cecil Rhodes.

58 Quoted in Rupert Lewis, *Marcus Garvey: anti-colonial champion* (London, Karia Press, 1987), p. 234.

59 See, e.g., Brian Simon, *The Two Nations and the Educational Structure 1780–1870* (London, Lawrence & Wishart, 1974); Henry E. Cowper, *British Education, Public and Private, and the British Empire 1880–1930*, PhD Thesis, University of Edinburgh, 1979. General education in much of mainland Europe was superior to that in Britain at this time.

60 It was almost always 'English' and not 'British'; quite often it was explicitly 'Anglo-Saxon' superiority that was inculcated.

61 The importance and use of athleticism to governing empire is mentioned by many analysts of the Victorian public school. See, e.g., Jonathan Rutherford, *Forever England: reflections on masculinity and empire* (London, Lawrence & Wishart, 1997). Perhaps the first book on the uses of sport in the colonies is C. L. R. James, *Beyond a Boundary* (1963), recently reissued by Penguin.

62 G. Best, 'Militarism and the Victorian public school', in B. Simon and I. Bradley (eds), *The Victorian Public School* (Dublin, Gill & Macmillan, 1975), p. 144. If the 'commerce' was lucrative enough, such susceptibilities were ignored. For example, sixty-four public school graduates worked for the East India Company in the period 1809–1850. (Bernard Cohn, 'Recruitment and training of British civil servants in India', in R. Braibanti, *Asiatic Bureaucratic Systems Emergent from the British Imperial Tradition* (Durham, NC, Duke University Press, 1966), chapter 3.

63 Robert Roberts, *Classic Slum* (London, 1973), p. 142.

64 Chancellor, op. cit., n. 53, p. 118. At first this 'typical Englishman' was only from the upper class; as exigencies changed, the model was imposed on all classes.

65 K. Castle, *Britannia's Children* (Manchester, Manchester University Press, 1996), pp. 7–8. See also A. P. Thornton, *The Imperial Idea and its Enemies* (London, Macmillan, 1966), pp. 89–92.

66 On geography texts, see Teresa Ploszajska, *Geographical Education, Empire and Citizenship* (Liverpool, Hope University College, 1999).

67 Racial imagery was also abundant in the 'readers' used to teach literacy. The advertisement for E. W. Kemple's *A Coon Alphabet* (*New Age*, 1898) quoted a review in the *St James Gazette*: 'a clever and amusing illustrated book for the child, which will also please their elders. Its nigger antics and humour are original as well as diverting.'

68 Chancellor, op. cit., n. 53, p. 22; Castle, op. cit., n. 65, pp. 14, 22, 25. See also C. H. Philips (ed.), *Historians of India, Pakistan and Ceylon: part II* (London, OUP, 1996), especially chapters 17, 25, 27 and 28.

69 Quoted by Frances Lawrence, 'Textbooks' in William Lamont, *The Realities of Teaching History: beginnings* (London, Chatto & Windus for Sussex University Press, 1972) pp. 121–2. Sir Charles Oman was Chichele Professor of Modern History at Oxford University.

70 Professor Meiklejohn's series: *Outlines of the History of England and Great Britain* (London, A. M. Holder, 1895), pp. 75–6.

71 Farrar in Michael D. Biddiss, *Images of Race* (Leicester, Leicester University Press, 1979), pp. 143, 147–8.

72 J.A. Mangan, '"The grit of our forefathers": invented traditions, propaganda and imperialism', in John M. MacKenzie (ed.), *Imperialism and Popular Culture* (Manchester, Manchester University Press, 1986), pp.120–1. On the effects of such education on those who went out to rule empire, see, e.g., C. Allen (ed.) *Tales from the Dark Continent* (London, Andre Deutsch, 1979).

73 On the racial views of other academics and some eminent Victorians, see K. K. Aziz, *The British in India* (New Delhi, Indian Institute of Applied Political Research 1988), chapter 3 and Douglas A. Lorimer, *Colour, Class and the Victorians* (Leicester, Leicester University Press, 1978).

74 G. Wheatcroft, *The Randlords* (New York, Touchstone Books, 1985), p. 139. Ruskin's pro-working-class, philanthropic but racist philosophy is echoed today by left-wing historians whose books on the British working class usually omit all mention of Black peoples.

75 By 'barbaric', one presumes that Sir John meant the North African ('Moorish') conquerors who ruled for 700 years.

76 Sir J. R. Seeley, *The Expansion of England* (London, Macmillan, 1894), pp. 138, 185. This book sold 80,000 copies in its first two years of publication. (H. John Field, *Toward a Programme of Imperial Life* (Westport, CT, Greenwood Press, 1982), p. 41). See Peter Burroughs, 'John Robert Seeley and British Imperial History', *Journal of Imperial & Commonwealth History*, (Vol. 1, 1973), pp. 191–211. Burroughs does not mention Seeley's racism but does quote from contemporary reviews, e.g., of *Expansion* in *Macmillan's Magazine* (February 1884), p. 242: 'It has helped and will further help, to well a sentiment that is already slowly rising

to full flood.' In his *Oceanea* (1886), Seeley wrote that the Maoris lived in 'animal sloth and indulgence . . . It is the with wild races of human beings as with wild animals . . . those only will survive who can domesticate themselves into servants of the modern forms of social development.' (pp. 257–8)

77 J. A. Froude, *The English in the West Indies* (London, Longmans, Green & Co, 1888), pp. 105, 252, 319 and *English Seamen in the Sixteenth Century*, (London, 1896) (lectures delivered in Oxford 1893–4). Froude was a friend of Joseph Chamberlain's.

78 The most comprehensive book on this subject is John M. MacKenzie, *Propaganda and Empire: the manipulation of British public opinion 1880–1960* (Manchester, Manchester University Press, 1984).

79 While Darwin appeared to hold no racist views in 1859, by 1871 in the *Descent of Man* he said he would prefer to be related to baboons than a 'savage who delights to torture his enemies, offers up bloody sacrifices without remorse, treats his wives like slaves, knows no decency and is haunted by the grossest superstitions'. (Patrick Brantlinger, *Rule of Darkness: British literature and imperialism* (Ithaca, NY, Cornell University Press, 1988), p. 187.

80 See, e.g., C. H. Lyons, *To Wash an Aethiop White: British ideas about Black African educability 1530–1960*, (New York, 1975).

81 Richard Drayton, *Nature's Government* (New Haven, CT, Yale University Press, 2000). See also Nancy Stepan, *The Idea of Race in Science: Great Britain 1800–1960* (London, Macmillan, 1982).

82 Trevor R. Reese, *The History of the Royal Commonwealth Society 1868–1968* (London, OUP, 1968), p. 16.

83 On Hunt and others, see Christine Bolt, *Victorian Attitudes to Race* (London, Routledge and Kegan Paul, 1971).

84 Paul Crook, 'Social Darwinism and British "New Imperialism": second thoughts', *The European Legacy* (Vol. 3, no. 1, 1998).

85 See, e.g.. Richard Price, 'Social status and jingoism', in G. Crossick (ed.), *The Lower Middle Class in Britain 1870–1914* (London, Croom Helm, 1977), pp. 89–112; J. A. Hobson, *The Psychology of Jingoism* (London, 1901).

86 Meath, ex-Eton and the Foreign Office, belonged to numbers of imperialist bodies and was an active proselytiser for empire in the public schools.

87 Mary Debenham, *Empire Day: a dialogue for children* (London, nd). See also H. Drake, *The British Empire and What it Stands For* (London, Royal Empire Society, nd). For a wonderful description of similar celebrations in Barbados in the 1930s, see George Lamming, *In the Castle of my Skin* (London, Michael Joseph, 1953), pp. 36 et seq.

88 Robert MacDonald, *Sons of Empire* (Toronto, Toronto University Press, 1993).

89 John Springall, *Youth, Empire and Society* (London, Croom Helm, 1977), p. 14.

90 See Brian Stanley, *The Bible and the Flag: Protestant missions and British imperialism in the nineteenth and twentieth centuries*, (Apollos, 1990); Andrew Porter, 'Cultural imperialism and the Protestant missionary enterprise 1780–1914', *Journal of Imperial & Commonwealth History* (Vol. 25, no. 3, 1997), pp. 367–91.

91 Brantlinger, op. cit., n. 79, pp. 180–1.

92 M. A. S. Barber, *Missionary Tales for Little Listeners* (London, Nisbet & Co, 1840). There appears to be no research on missionaries' sermons in Britain.

93 Halévy, quoted in David Thomson, *England in the Nineteenth Century* (1950), (Harmondsworth, Penguin, 1971), p. 204. According to Dunae (n. 95 below), Henty was a shareholder in the Transvaal Gold Mines.

94 W. H. Fitchett, *Deeds That Won the Empire* (London, Smith, Elder & Co, 1910), pp. v–vi. This was the twenty-sixth edition.

95 See Louis James, 'Tom Brown's imperialist sons', *Victorian Studies* (Vol. 17, no. 1, 1973), pp. 89–99; Patrick A Dunae, 'Boys' literature and the idea of empire 1870–1914', *Victorian Studies* (Vol. 24, no. 1, 1980), pp. 105–21.

96 Quotation from Daniel Bivong, *Desire and Contradiction: imperial visions and domestic debates in Victorian literature* (Manchester, Manchester University Press, 1990); see also B. V. Street, *The Savage in Literature* (London, Routledge & Kegan Paul, 1975). There are now many books investigating the connections between imperialism/racism and literature; for a Europe-wide perspective, see Hugh Ridley, *Images of Imperial Rule* (London, Croom Helm, 1983). See also Rana Kabbani, *Imperial Fictions: Europe's Myths of Orient* (London, Pandora, 1986).

97 Dudley Kidd, The *Essential Kaffir* (London, A. C. Black, 1925), pp. 395–407.

98 On Thackeray, who was also anti-semitic, see John Sutherland, 'Thackeray as Victorian racialist', *Essays in Criticism* (Vol. 20, no. 4, 1970), pp. 441–50.

99 Denis Judd, *Empire* (London, HarperCollins, 1996), p. 67. On press reactions to the Morant Bay Rebellion in Jamaica in 1865, see Bolt, op. cit., n. 83, chapter 3.

100 The *Daily Mail* was the first newspaper intended for mass circulation. Its stated aim was to be 'the embodiment and mouthpiece of the Imperial idea . . . the articulate voice of British progress and domination . . . We know that the advance of the Union Jack means protection for weaker races, justice for the oppressed, liberty for the downtrodden . . . It is for the power, the greatness, the supremacy of the Empire that we have stood.' (*Daily Mail,* fourth anniversary issue, 1900, quoted in J. Harvey and K. Hood, *The British State* (New York, International Publishers, 1959), p. 262). Lord Beaverbrook's *Daily Express* from 1913 adopted the *Mail's* techniques and purpose.

101 On music halls, see Penny Summerfield, 'Patriotism and empire', in MacKenzie, 1986, op. cit., n. 72; on art and artists, see '"Up Guards and at them": British imperialism in popular art', ibid.; on the stage, Ben Shephard, 'Showbiz imperialism', ibid.

102 Five and a half million attended the 1886 'Colonial and Indian' exhibition and twenty-seven million the 1924/1925 Empire Exhibition. (MacKenzie, 1984, op. cit., n. 78, p. 100).

103 MacKenzie, ibid., p. 113.

104 See Paul S. Landau and D. Kaspin (eds), *Images and Empires: visuality in colonial and post-colonial Africa* (forthcoming); Brian Street, 'British popular anthropology: exhibiting and photographing the Other', in E. Edwards (ed.), *Anthropology and Photography 1860–1921* (New Haven, CT, Yale University Press, 1992, pp. 122–131 (the quotation is from p. 122). James R. Ryan noted in his *Picturing Empire* (London, Reaktion Books, 1997), p. 219, that 'it would be wrong to exaggerate the coherence and effectiveness of photography as a vehicle of imperial repression'.

105 Cowper, op. cit., n. 59, p. 238.

106 Quoted in Henry Pelling, *Popular Politics and Society in Late Victorian Britain* (1968) (London, Macmillan, 1979), p. 85.

107 We can catch a glimpse of the indoctrination used by the army from the recruitment handbooks used in India. These often differentiated between the light-skinned Aryans and the 'darker skinned lower types'. The 'martial races' were usually described as being of Aryan descent and recruitment was to be, as far as possible, from 'racially pure' Aryans. (David Omissi, *The Sepoy and the Raj* (London, Macmillan, 1994), p. 32.) George Orwell, recalling his days as a police officer in Burma in the 1920s, wrote of the British soldiers in Burma who 'develop an attitude towards the "nigger" which is far more brutal than that of the officials or businessmen'. (Bernard Crick, *George Orwell: a life* (Harmondsworth, Penguin, 1982), p. 149.) See John M. MacKenzie (ed.), *Popular Imperialism and the Military* (Manchester, Manchester University Press, 1992). Lionel Caplan, in '"Bravest of the

brave": representations of the "Gurkha" in British military writing', *Modern Asian Studies* (Vol. 25, no. 3, 1991), pp. 571–97) presents a very interesting analysis, following Edward Said's seminal *Orientalism*, 1978. See also Said's *Culture and Imperialism* (London, Chatto & Windus, 1993). On the barbarities of the conquest – that is, the 'civilising mission', see, e.g., Lawrence James, ' "The White Man's Burden": Imperial wars in the 1890s', *History Today* (August 1992). See also the pro-imperialist *Victoria's Enemies*, by Donald Featherstone, published in 1989.

108 Richard T. Lapiere, 'Race prejudice', *Social Forces* (Vol. 7, 1928), pp. 102–9.

109 G. Green, 'Racial prejudice among school children', *Geography* (Vol. 16, 1931), pp. 50–1. Curiously, Iona and Peter Opie record no racist chants in their *Lore and Language of Schoolchildren* (London, OUP, 1959). Yet, when I asked just one Black person whether she remembered any, Josephine Florent (now aged 89) recalled the following from her days at Netly Street Primary School, north London: 'Blackie, blackie weasel/ Stick her on a needle/ If she hollers let her go/ Blackie, blackie weasel'. This was chanted while the children circled around her. 'I was terrified', Josephine recalls. (Interview, London, 6 June 1999.)

110 See Marika Sherwood, 'Lynching in Britain', *History Today* (March 1999) and 'Engendering racism: history and history teachers in English schools', *Research in African Literatures* (Vol. 30, no. 1, Spring 1999), pp. 184–203.

111 Most 'coloured' seamen were in fact British; see Marika Sherwood, 'Race, nationality and employment among Lascar seamen 1660–1945', *New Community* (Vol. 17, no. 3, 1991), pp. 229–44.

112 S. G. Searle, 'Eugenics and politics in Britain in the 1930s', *Annals of Science* (Vol. 36, 1979), pp. 159–69. See also Eleazar Barkan, *The retreat of scientific racism* (Cambridge, CUP, 1992). Julian Huxley was knighted in 1958 and had been the first director-general of UNESCO. This great populariser of science, scion of a most eminent family, after a visit to West Africa, described Kano in northern Nigeria as a 'barbaric mud-walled city' which was divided not into streets, but 'burrows'. All Africans were 'inherently cheerful'. (Julian Huxley, 'How West Africa is governed', *Picture Post* (18 August 1945), pp. 20–3).

113 Rachel Fleming, 'Human Hybrids', *Eugenics Review* (Vol. 21, 1929–30), pp. 257–63.

114 M. E. Fletcher, *Report on an Investigation into the Colour Problem in Liverpool and other Ports* (Liverpool, Association for the Welfare of Half-caste Children, 1930), p. 28; R. M. Fleming, 'Anthropological studies of children', *Eugenics Review* (Vol. 18, 1926/27), pp. 294–301.

115 Quoted in Joanna Bourke, *Working-Class Cultures in Britain 1890–1960* (London, Routledge, 1994). The series was called 'The Colour Question'.

116 J. L. Keith, quoted in Sherwood, 1999, op. cit., n. 110, p. 193.

117 H. B. Gray, *The Public Schools and the Empire* (London, Williams & Norgate, 1913), p. 198.

118 *Daily Telegraph* (28 January 1927), quoted in Cowper, op. cit., n. 59, p. 265. The national curriculum for schools in 1999 reflects the same policy.

119 Sherwood, 1999, op. cit., n. 110.

120 Published by Pilot Press, London; the quotations are from p. 20.

121 On the present state of textbooks, see Marika Sherwood, 'Sins of omission and commission', *Multicultural Teaching* (Spring 1999), pp. 14–22.

HAZEL WATERS

Putting on 'Uncle Tom' on the Victorian stage

If theatre was the mass entertainment medium of the Victorian age, one of its biggest popular hits was the importation from America, in the late 1830s, of the bizarre figure of 'Jim Crow' and his song and dance act. Crow, the creation of the white American actor T. D. Rice, and based, so the story goes, on the shuffling dance and crooning song of a crippled black ostler Rice had witnessed, was held to be a genuine representation of the American black – and, as such, not simply an inferior sort of human being, but, rather, outside the human species altogether. One theatre critic 'presume[d]' Rice's 'representation of a Yankee nigger' to be 'correct' on the grounds that it was 'so utterly unlike any other human being, either black or white, that we can hardly doubt its being like the race, or the individual, it is meant for'.[1]

With his coal-black face, eye rolling, frenzied dancing, weird gesticulation, 'slave' dialect, parodic costume and flattery of his audience, Jim Crow was an instant success in a medium always hungry for novelty. Crow songs were whistled in the streets, child beggars did Crow routines for pennies, audiences packed Rice's twice-nightly shows and Crow's distorted figure and grinning face adorned playbills, sold song-sheets, cigars and 'Jim Crow' hats. Even the Duke of Devonshire was said to have had himself taught to 'jump Jim Crow'. Though British audiences had long been familiar with the stereotype of the vengeful

---

Hazel Waters is currently researching the black presence on the nineteenth-century stage, as a part-time student at Birkbeck College, London. She was awarded the Harold and Jean Brooks prize for studies in drama, for 2000.

Race & Class
Copyright © 2001 Institute of Race Relations
Vol. 42(3): 29–48 [0306-3968(200101)42:3; 29–48; 016112]

or wicked African (present in the drama from the seventeenth century onwards[2]) or the comic black servant (from the eighteenth century onwards) and had even been introduced, via the comedian Charles Mathews, to a comic stereotype of the American black in the mid-1820s, nothing had caught the popular imagination quite so forcefully as the grotesque Crow. Crow flourished on the stage from 1836 to the early 1840s – with another brief flurry in the late 1840s – and thereafter escaped into popular entertainment generally, in minstrelsy and black-face, on the streets and in the music halls, till he died a lingering and protracted death in the early twentieth century. He did not pass on, however, without leaving a legacy, in an area where one might not initially expect to find it.

He was succeeded on the stage by a racial gallery of types, from (black-skinned) Uncle Tom and Topsy, to (light-skinned) Eliza and George Harris. For, after minstrelsy, the next popular 'black' vogue was for Uncle Tom. That Tom's and Topsy's names are instantly and generally recognised, while the latter two are not, is suggestive of the racialised cultural climate into which they (and we) were born. But what was the link between Crow and Tom? What was the line of development and what did it signify?

To begin to answer these questions, it is necessary to look at another mid-century vogue, running alongside that for minstrelsy; a vogue for tales of slavery told by ex-slaves themselves.[3] It is this that provides the context for Uncle Tom's success. Just as the racism of the Jim Crow variety found a ready market in a race-conscious England fascinated by all things American, so the abolitionist movement now coming to a crescendo in America and spearheaded by black abolitionists them-selves also found a ready and fascinated audience in England. In the thirty years before the American Civil War, every major black leader visited the UK, with more coming in the period 1848–52 than at any other time. Many performed lengthy and sustained lecture tours across the whole country, and a figure with the presence and eloquence of Frederick Douglass, for instance, was lionised at every level of society.[4] (He humorously complained that he was not really quite black enough for English society, but passed muster by making his hair as woolly as possible.[5]) At another level, the lectures of Henry 'Box' Brown, who displayed a panorama depicting the abuses of slavery and who made his appearance on stage in the very box in which he had escaped, veered towards stage performances. As the *New York Express* sourly commented:

> The mother country, of late years, has signalized itself particularly in the great delight it has taken to avail itself of every opportunity to foster, and feed, and flatter, runaway American negroes . . . Persians with long beards, – Turks with long pipes – Chinese, with long tails,

and North American Indians, with *not very long* blankets are constantly succeeding one another in the *salons* or at the tables of the *haut ton* . . . Nothing goes down, now . . . so well as the genuine black.[6]

And slave narratives, with their graphic accounts of terrible cruelties and harrowing escapes, sold in their thousands. No doubt part of their appeal was their sensationalism, albeit under sober guise. But they also appealed to the powerful, abolitionist thrust in English culture and thinking, which, emerging at the end of the eighteenth century, continued to be a powerful force through the abolition of the slave trade (1807), the abolition of slavery (1833), of 'apprenticeship' (virtual slavery) in the West Indies (1838) and now received a new boost with the campaign to abolish slavery in America.[7] (Abolitionism should not, of course, be confused with racial egalitarianism.)

'Select scenes and join them together'

The climate was therefore ripe for Harriet Beecher Stowe's dramatic and vivid indictment of the institution of slavery, *Uncle Tom's Cabin*, to become a runaway success on both sides of the Atlantic when it was published in 1852.[8] And the theatre, that ready mirror of popular response, quickly caught on to the appeal of 'Uncle Tom', both in America and in Britain. Versions of it were first performed in London in September 1852, only a few months after the novel had come out in England, at the Standard, the Olympic and the Victoria. By December 1852, it was being played at eleven theatres in the capital.[9] In Birmingham, it played to packed houses even as Beecher Stowe began a successful lecture tour from there. According to the popular and prolific playwright, Fitzball:

> The publication of 'Uncle Tom's Cabin', in the deservedly popular production of Mrs. Stowe, set all the managers mad to produce it on the stage. Every theatre nearly produced its own version. I don't know whose was the best. I was engaged by three managers to write three distinct pieces, which I did to the best of my ability, as it was only to select scenes and join them together.[10]

Part of the appeal of Stowe's novel for dramatists was, indeed, that much of its racy, naturalistic dialogue could be transferred wholesale to the stage – hence, in versions that differed widely as to their overall thrust, plot outline, or over which characters were included and which omitted, the same passages of dialogue recur. The novel itself abounded in strong melodramatic situations and pictures – notably, the escape of the enslaved mother, Eliza, her child in her arms, over the frozen Ohio river; the whipping of Uncle Tom and a female slave by the brutal slave-owner Simon Legree; the almost unmasking of the escaped slave George (Eliza's husband) in a Kentucky tavern while he is on the run; his heroic stand-off across a rocky mountain pass with the slave-hunters; the slave auction that separates a mother and her beautiful young daughter; the heavenly tableau of the saintly white child, Eva St Clare, and the black Christ figure, Tom. And of course slavery itself, as a theme, offered huge dramatic potential, with its stark (black and white) struggle of good against evil, of the humble oppressed against a tyrannical oppressor, its narratives of bravery against all odds, daring escapes, brutalities, with the ultimate prize of freedom as the goal.

It is necessary to consider the novel in some detail, since there are crucial aspects of it that were impossible to stage and others which easily lent themselves to drama. This imbalance led to an arbitrary representation which, while the thematic structure of the novel *could* have led to a portrayal of Tom and other figures that restored some element of human dignity to the black figure (dignity that Crow had so unequivocally trampled on), what actually resulted was the generalisation of the Crow image to the black male character as a whole.

Stowe is concerned in the novel to depict the evil of slavery as an institution – not just its excesses, or the abuses it inspired, but its systemic wickedness. At the very core of the novel is a profoundly Christian value system in which all souls are of equal worth before God – from the degraded Prue, a 'breeder' robbed of all children to whom she has given birth, even the very last, to the brutalised Sambo and Quimbo, Legree's slave slave-drivers, to (white) little Eva. Even Legree himself – a powerfully drawn character whose immediate impact is that of physical threat – has the potential for redemption, but it is a potential on which he resolutely turns his back. The action of the novel turns on the separate escapes of George Harris (to rid himself of an abusive master and live, with his family, as a free man) and his wife Eliza (to save their child from being sold) and the refusal of Uncle Tom to act likewise – leading to his sale, first to a benevolent but indolent master, St Clare, and then to Legree, at whose hands he dies.

But, if all souls are of equal value, and the evil of slavery is that it substitutes man's ownership of man for God's relationship with the individual, all the characters are not of equal weight. A definite race hierarchy operates within the novel – to each race is assigned its own particular gifts and qualities which it is incumbent upon it to develop. Thus, to the African, the humblest and most docile of peoples, is the God-given task of serving God through missionary work and the practice of religion. For the dominant Anglo-Saxon race, on the other hand, it is necessary to show mercy, nobler to 'protect the feeble than to oppress them'.[11] Hence, throughout all the dramatic and exciting incident of the novel, the detailed material description of daily life –

and the insight that the anti-slavery of the northern states can mask a physical repugnance to the black – there is also a detailed racial schema in operation.

The main protagonists of the novel, the husband and wife escapees Eliza and George Harris, are both handsome, light-skinned individuals. So much so that, when George is on the run and a poster has been circulated with his description, he disguises himself by *darkening* his complexion with a little walnut juice, so as to look Spanish, and dyeing his hair. They are resourceful and determined – Eliza's strength deriving from her Christian belief and her motherly love and George's from his knowledge that he is his 'master's' equal, if not superior, and burning desire to live in freedom. He is the embodiment of manliness, she of womanliness. George's passion is counterbalanced by Eliza's counselling of patience and submission to God's will. The apogee of Christian fortitude, however, is Tom himself, the icon of the abolitionist medallion 'Am I not a man and a brother?' set in motion. He is the total abstraction of Christ-like forgiveness, on earth to suffer and resign his spirit to God's will. A purely moral emblem, he plays scarcely any structural role in forwarding the action of the novel; his resistance, while of the highest moral order, consisting as it does of refusing to obey the will of his owner over that of God, is passive, spiritual and results in his transcendence into a Christ figure. In dying a death of agony, he is the instrument of saving the souls of others, the brutalised slaves of Legree. His spirituality, won through pain, is of the profoundest, but he has also a white counterpart, the natural saint, little Eva, daughter of St Clare. Both are children in God, both travel part of their spiritual journey together. Eva is too good to live, Tom too good not to suffer and die. And against little Eva is set another child, Topsy, the black embodiment of heathen ignorance and mischief, quick and cunning, yet, under the influence of Eva, capable of good.

'Wesleyan talkee talkee'

The action, the vivid colloquial speech, not only of the slaves but of the slave traders and 'men of business' could all be and were, with varying degrees of success, translated from the novel on to the stage. But the book's spiritual heart was incapable of embodiment within the confines of melodrama, and not only because of the prohibition on representing Christian iconography on the stage. Tom's journey is an inner one; it could not be expressed in the powerful, declamatory and expository style of nineteenth-century melodrama, which was suited to strong emotion and exciting physical action, but not to the quieter depths of the metaphysical. While the character of Tom 'works' within the novel because of the profundity and sincerity of its Christianity, it becomes a meaningless nonsense, or worse, as soon as he steps from those pages.

The impossibility of representing Uncle Tom on stage was recognised in a lengthy review by *The Spectator* of the version written by Mark Lemon and Tom Taylor, entitled *Slave Life; or, Uncle Tom's Cabin*, played at the Adelphi.[12] It was a relative latecomer to the field, being first performed on 29 November 1852. Dramatically, it is one of the most coherent versions – 'a perfectly inoffensive drama, of considerable constructive merit' – though differing drastically from the novel:

> Not one of the qualities which strike the heart in Mrs Stowe's novel is preserved in the play; but then . . . not one of those qualities was capable of stage representation. The soul of Uncle Tom floats far above, and in Wesleyan talkee-talkee repudiates their alliance: so we must not only be satisfied with obtaining a slice of his mortal frame, but must commend the authors for the admirable craftsmanship with which they have subdued their stubborn material.[13]

And, indeed, the 'characterisation' of Uncle Tom varies wildly in all the plays, linked only by its unlikeness to Stowe's characterisation. In the novel, his strength and saintliness, because of Stowe's utter sincerity, do carry conviction – though, as I have argued, as soon as he steps out of that intense atmosphere, he crumples into cardboard. Therefore, what is suggested in the plays is all the more revealing of the matrix of racialised beliefs, attitudes and stereotypes which were compounded in this latest interpretation of black-white relations.

The very first version to be staged, *Uncle Tom's Cabin; or, the Negro Slave* (at the Standard, 8 September 1852[14]) foregrounds a white character who scarcely even features in this panoramic novel. The saviour of all, at crucial points in the narrative (which contains the standard elements of the separate escapes of Eliza and George, the refusal to escape of Tom, the assistance given by the Quakers to the fugitives and Tom's sale to Legree), is the good-hearted, brave, down-to-earth Van Tromp, a former slave-owner who has seen the light. It is Van Tromp who fights off the slave-hunters Marks and Loker, Van Tromp who tells George how to escape by riding a log down the rapids of the Ohio river, Van Tromp who is almost killed by bloodhounds when assisting George, Van Tromp into whose hands falls all the estate – and slaves – of Legree, and Van Tromp who, of course, makes all right.

In this can be seen refracted the paternalistic prejudices formed throughout the course of abolitionism. Lorimer has argued how abolitionism, in the persistence with which it pursued its case and under the necessity of pleading its cause, also served to entrench a sentimentalised racial stereotype of the black.[15] And the Standard's version of Uncle Tom (a confusing potboiler in terms of its action) falls into that vision. Thus, Tom himself displays almost nothing of the exaggerated dialect that subsequent versions assigned to him. Instead, he retains more than a little of the noble African, wrenched from his homeland, that had long been a familiar figure on the English stage. He is dignified with the slave-hunter Loker:

> *Loker*: Fine times when freedom of speech is granted to a black face . . .
> *Tom*: Chance may have given you a power over the limb but Heaven gives power to that and freedom to that which they can never fetter, the mind.

And, when Van Tromp shakes his hand, Tom is moved to reflect:

> Tisn't everyone would give his hand to a Man of Colour, many have an antipathy to Black . . . If all were as liberal minded as he, he who has left the dusty sons of Africa would never feel the Racking Chain that binds them. Alas, there are but few, but those few, like the distant storm that gathers in strength and power as it comes, may work the good they labour for – and, rushing as the tempest, sweep from the earth's fair surface the name of slaves.[16] (punctuation added)

This image of Tom is still extant in the curious version produced one week later by Eliza Vincent at the Victoria, on 15 September 1852 (*Uncle Tom's Cabin; or, the Fugitive Slave!*[17]). But the image is already showing signs of its future development. Tom's language veers crazily in register and tone. Here is how he greets Eliza when she comes to his cabin to warn of the impending sale:

> *Tom*: Ha that haggard face – and wild dark eye tell a tale of suffering – I wish to ask but dread to know the cause . . .

On the other hand, when he, George and Eliza are all on board a slave ship:

> *Tom*: I tell you George dar is hope . . . on de oder side of de riber you would be safe . . . if you can get into de boat wid your Lizy . . .[18]

In this version, Tom has little scope for developing his persona, his role being largely limited to one or two speeches expressing moral defiance of Legree, for which he is whipped to death, off stage.

But the first of Fitzball's versions is another matter (*Uncle Tom's Cabin*, Royal Olympic Theatre, 20 September 1852[19]). No longer is it for Tom to give vent to the injustice of slavery – that is now the sole province of the light-skinned George Harris. Instead, our first encounter with him, in the snug, almost fairy-tale, confines of his cabin, snow falling thickly outside, is this:

> *Tom*: He! He! He! Well 'm do lub massa. Him nebber tink to part Tom from him childers: Tom lay down him life for good kind

> massa . . . dere nebber wur sich massa an sich missus. I do tink dem
> nabber sell 'mself . . . *dear* massa . . .

And his reaction, when he finds out he is to be sold:

> *Tom*: No; no: I ain't going: Let Lizy go . . . tant in natur for her to
> stay . . . I must be sold to pay masser's debt, or all tings, may go to
> rack an ruin: Poor massar and missis, turn'd out o their comforble
> home . . . Masser ant to blame Chloe; he'll take care o you and de
> childer when Tom's gone; and if Masser's in trouble, Tom's willin
> to go – *die* for m (dashing away tears).[20]

This is Tom full-fledged, and is the image of Tom which, by and large,
henceforth pertains, though laid on more thickly here than in some
versions. ('Uncle Tom, a quiet, low comedy part with more than a
dash of sentiment' was the way *The Era* characterised it in one
review.[21]) And nothing could be more expressive of racial inferiority
than this unctuous dependence on the very institution to which the
slave's life was forfeit. Here, the black is rendered sentimental and
pathetic to an unprecedented degree and we can perhaps see in
Tom's speeches the conjunction of two projections of racialised
belief. On the one hand, the sentimental pathos of Tom is on a continuum with the kneeling, manacled slave begging to be recognised as
a man; the object of white pity and paternalism. But, at the same
time, in his actual use of language (the child-like self-referral in the
third person, the use of all purpose 'm' as a pronoun), and especially
in his occasional more comic moments, he is a re-presentation of the
grotesque Jim Crow.

His by-play with his garrulous wife, Chloe, for example, depends on
the familiar notion of the bathetic nature of black love and the black
family: their children, tucked up asleep are, in Chloe's words, 'like so
many innocent black coopids atop o white clouds: Only listen how
beauty em's a snorin . . .' And the image of domestic happiness
which is about to be sundered by the sale of Tom is presented like this:

> *Tom*: . . . massa an missy won [sic] flesh, in blood: An arn't you an I
> same metal. Only 'm do think, you most beautifulest and lobberly
> woman, eber lib'd out o paradise (kisses her) He! He!
> *Chloe*: Oh Tom you're a duck, dat's what 'm is . . . (Tom hugs her,
> candle in hand)
> *Tom*: Oh Cloe! Cloe! m's Wenus an . . . al de greases [i.e., graces][22]

(Greasiness was a common stereotype of black skin and expression
of repugnance to it.) It is worth noting that, about a decade and a
half earlier, at the height of the Jim Crow craze, Fitzball had portrayed
a demonic black villain in *The Negro of Wapping* who was finally
located firmly in the mould of the vengeful African cast into slavery.

Nothing of that now remains, although at the very last Tom (who in this version does not die) is allowed a moment of dignity. As Tom, his wife and children sink to their knees together with cries of joy and George, Eliza, their child and Mr Shelby enter, forming a picture, Tom speaks thus:

> *Tom*: Merciful power! You have not forgotten, look down and witness the mingled gratitude of the poor slave. (Moment of devotion in which the picture is contemplated in silence: all the men take off their hats).[23]

In the Lemon and Taylor version, on the other hand, as *The Spectator* pointed out, Tom is almost elided,[24] being more or less confined to expressing the morality of the play, which for the most part he does in standard English, only lapsing into more colloquial slave dialect in the bosom of his family.[25]

Why not dis nigger?

Tom, though, is not the only representation of the black in these plays. The Standard's version opens – as do a number of others – with another picture, familiar from the eighteenth century onwards, of the happy plantation scene. Here the scene is focused on the minor comical characters of Sam and Andy (an early version of Amos 'n' Andy?). Sam is the stereotype of minstrelsy, his stupidity matched only by his self-importance, his inability to use language matched by his pride in his 'speechifying'; Andy is his more clued-up sidekick. It is they who locate the audience in this other world of the plantation, they who confirm the audience's preconceived expectations of slave life and mores. Sam is all for defending the slaves' rights:

> *Sam*: You see fellow countrymen, you see what's this Chile up to, it's for fending yer all, yes all of yer, I'll stand up for your rights, I'll fend em to my last breath . . . boys like you Andy means well but they can't be spected to collusitate the great principal [sic] of action. (punctuation added)[26]

That Sam is quite prepared to make a genuine search for the missing Eliza, in this version as in all others, and enhance his own standing by finding her and bringing her back, exposes the hollowness of his boasts: 'Well it's an ill wind that blows nowise, dat are a fact, well of course dere is room for some nigger to be up, and why not dis Nigger.' (punctuation added)[27] Only when Andy points out that 'Missee don't want her catched' does Sam change his tune. Then, in the manner of comic servants everywhere, he manages to thwart Eliza's recapture while pretending to aid it.

All this is, of course, in Stowe's novel, detailed at great length, and she makes clear that part of Sam's 'front' is just that, a face to meet the faces that he meets. He is unctuous with his deeply religious mistress, bragging before his fellow slaves, and, by playing the part of the deferential, stupid slave, performs a classic double take on the slave-trader Haley in the search for Eliza that enables Eliza to gain enough time to make her escape. While Stowe looks askance at her creation for his fundamental dishonesty, it is possible for a later generation to recognise Sam's ability for 'puttin' on massa', as a viable slave strategy, even though he is cast within the bounds of stereotype. But to develop too far the notion of a subtle, manipulative Sam, working white society for his own purposes, would weaken the concept of a racialised hierarchy (albeit inverted by what Yellin terms a 'Christian transvaluation'[28]) on which the novel depends. And it would run counter to the rigid racialism expressed in the plays.

On stage, Sam and Andy remain black buffoons to a greater extent than in the novel. Generally, their function in the overall action is greater and Sam's use of language is given much play. In the version by Eliza Vincent, Sam, as well as taking the limelight in the scene in which 'Lizzy' (as she is in this version) is discovered to have gone missing, is also shown having a quarrel with MilkWhite (a very minor figure in the novel) over her infatuation with the white comic figure, Tom Tickler. The dialogue between Sam and MilkWhite makes the usual obvious pun and has the characteristics of 'minstrel' speech:

> *Sam*: So Miss MilkWhite you may turn black if you please – and you may turn de corner an I care a button – you no get ober me dat way howsomdever.
> *MilkWhite*: Massa Tickler am got a wife – but if she dies, him says – I shall be Mrs. Tickler.
> *Sam*: Hold your tongue MilkWhite and go and do 'um work.[29]

There is an echo here of the type of 'Ethiopian opera' that was so popular from the days of Crow onwards; its humour lying in the premise that a) romance between blacks was funny and b) their pretensions were even funnier. Often such 'romances' revolved around the rivalry between a grotesque black (like Crow) and a 'dandy' type, aping his betters, for the affections of their beloved – who just wants to do as well for herself as possible. And, indeed, while *Uncle Tom* was playing to packed houses, just such a piece, G. H. George's rhyming doggerel with songs attached, *A Colour'd Commotion*, was playing at the Strand.[30] The versions of Uncle Tom and their peculiarities of emphasis have to be seen in the wider context of a public taste by now familiarised to, and expectant of, a particular grotesque image of the American black.

Topsy is the other character type who falls into the category of the grotesque. Again, for the most part she is put on stage for her comical shock value as an expression of complete amorality. Most versions are content to reproduce extracts of dialogue, sometimes rather garbled, straight from the novel, in which Topsy steals ribbons from under her mistress's nose, is told to confess and so confesses to what she hasn't done. Topsy has no concept either of right or wrong, or of mother or father, having been raised by a 'speculator'. In the novel, her state of brutalised, heathen ignorance is a foil to the naturally profound moral sense of Eva and a comment on the evil of slavery's destruction of family life. In the plays, she is a brief black comic turn (Eva does not figure in most of them), much in the manner of Sam and Andy, but who plays no part in the action. She afforded a certain scope for effect to the actresses who played her, usually in a turban and freakish dress suggestive of the black child slave-servant of an earlier period.[31] Topsy's comic strangeness was popular, she could be comfortably laughed at, sealed off as she was from the rest of the moral universe. Only in Lemon and Taylor's version does she become a major figure: a sentimentalised and docile version of the character whose sharpness as a type stood out in the novel, she is smoothed off into the comic servant, aiding George's escape, helping reunite George and Eliza and thwarting Legree's plans. Her constant catchphrase, 'I's so wicked' is belied by her actions, but also serves to establish her inferior status. It was a change that was not altogether to the taste of *The Spectator*'s reviewer:

> We only wish they had abstained from making Topsey assume the disguise of a pert 'tiger'. The other personages of the piece exhibit the various actors in positions which we have seen over and over again; but *Topsey* as represented by Mrs. Keeley is one of those bold though highly-finished pictures of character which, however small, stand out from the general mass, and we regret to see it toned down into mere stage-conventionality.[32]

The Era was more wholehearted, praising: 'the surprising manner in which [Mrs Keeley] realized the conception of the author . . . As the negro girl, believing herself to be wicked, yet doing good, she was inimitable.'[33] Topsey has become not too unfamiliar, is held within the moral universe, albeit as an inferior.

The slave drama as domestic melodrama

Uncle Tom and Topsy have survived in the popular imagination because, for the most part, they fitted so well into the minstrelised vision of the Black. And slavery, passionately, if intermittently, denounced in drama from *Oroonoko* onwards, in terms of universal human values for its assault on the individual, has become an assault on liberty that is expressed, dramatically, as an assault on the family. Or rather, two families. There is the comical family of Uncle Tom; nearly every play has a scene in Tom's cabin, with black children hugger mugger, sometimes even being thrown food by their mother Chloe, who, however, hands it to the white son of the Shelby family, George. (The Shelbys own the plantation.) Tom, childlike himself, is nearly always shown being instructed in the art of writing by George. His admiration of George flatters the audience directly. 'How easy white folks always does things!' he exclaims.[34] No doubt, many of those who flocked to see *Uncle Tom* could not read or write either – but Tom assured them that they could, if they would. Out of all the incidents of the novel that were not dramatised, or only occasionally so, this is a constant and reflects, with a comfortable, patronising warmth, the basic inferiority of Tom's family. Only in the complete reworking of the novel by Lemon and Taylor is this altered to show Tom's children learning to write. In fact, their depiction of Uncle Tom's family life is more tender and natural than most. But Tom has a certain dignity accorded him here which is elsewhere denied him ('a passive black, always sinned against and never sinning'[35]).

And there is the almost white family of George and Eliza Harris and their son Harry. George and Eliza are married but unable to live together as man and wife and George, from being a skilled worker in a factory, is to be sent back to the plantation and forced to take another 'wife'. Hence his determination to escape to Canada. Then, when Harry is sold from Eliza, she too is forced to flee. Stowe's novel, with its emphasis on the family – from the central situation of George and Eliza, the separation of Tom, Chloe and their children to the story of the motherless and fatherless Topsy, to the sexual degradation of young women sold away from their mothers at auction – obviously lends itself to domestic melodrama of the most powerful nature. Indeed, the very characterisation falls neatly into place with all the stock types of the genre. There is Uncle Tom, a variant of the good old man; Eliza the virtuous heroine and mother, pursued by the villainous slave trader Haley, intent on breaking up the family unit for his own ends; George, the heroic husband, defying death for his wife and child; Sam, Andy, Topsy all, variously, comic servants.

Thus, in all the plays, Eliza's love for her child, that most sacred of domestic ties, is insisted on at every turn – to Mrs Budd (the ferryman's wife who, in some versions, helps Eliza to escape) to Mrs Bird (the kind-hearted senator's wife who takes her in) and in appeals to Legree or Haley. It is emphasised in the Lemon and Taylor adaptation, for example, which interpolates a scene where Eliza reads Harry a good night story as he falls asleep. Then, as she prepares to take him away, a lengthy passage details the small, domestic preparations she makes:

Eliza: Poor boy! poor boy! they have sold us, but your mother will save you yet. (*she places a toy upon the table*) That toy may keep him quiet should he be alarmed when I wake him. (*she goes to a cupboard, L., and opens it, then spreads out a handkerchief as though to form a bundle; she places cakes and fruit in it, listening every now and then*) He will need something before I shall dare to seek for shelter or refreshment. Where is his mantle? (*takes out a mantle and places it on the bed*) The night is frosty; poor fellow he may have far to travel. (*she takes out some articles of infant clothing, a lace cap and small frock*) Ah, this! (*from a box, R., she presses it to her lips*) Time was when I should have wept to have parted with this relic. They are too happy to be mourned for – all is ready. (*She rouses* HARRY.)[36]

Of course, the charm of this passage is that it is so simple and unaffected. Most of the plays are far more declamatory in style, and one Eliza even contemplates murdering her son to save him from his fate. But, while some versions allude to Tom's distress at the separation from his children, this is scarcely ever treated with anything like the sympathetic dignity evidenced in the preceding passage, and Tom's expressions of distress are generally contained within his status as a virtual simpleton.

In another significant departure from the novel, virtually nothing is made of what Stowe terms Tom's 'stubborn preference' for freedom. The Tom we see in virtually all the plays is only too happy to serve a (good) master – and willing to serve a bad. His black skin denotes the utmost servility. It is from the light-skinned George, rather, that the most bitterly felt denunciations of slavery emanate, often taken almost verbatim from the novel, but varying in their length and emphasis. Those denunciations either focus on the devastation slavery wreaks on the right to family life, thus emphasising the domestic theme, or, in an echo of earlier dramas, dwell on the nature of man and liberty. Nearly all have some version of the following:

Eliza: Oh George, your master –
George: My master! Master in what – am I not in form and strength his more than equal, in heart and intellect his superior? Although chance and law, unjust law, a law that every nation but our own despise, deny, gave power over me, 'tis but the Law of Man, the Law of Heaven, I feel, gives freedom to my soul and bids me burst the trammels that corrupt justice and despite power binds me in, bids me be as Heaven ordained. I should be free as air.[37] (punctuation added)

This is still redolent of the language of universalism and of the enlightenment, of earlier expressions of anti-slavery sentiment. Interestingly, it is George's language that comes closest to expressing those sentiments of revenge for the injustice done to the black protagonist that characterise earlier dramas that touch on slavery. Has the black avenger become the almost white one? Here is Fitzball reworking the same theme (after a passage in which even Eliza has expressed the view that the Almighty 'ordains, for some great end that the African *should be* a slave'):

> *George*: Master! Who made him my master? What right has he to me? . . . In strength: in intellect I am infinitely his superior: yet I am driven about by the command of such a thing . . . when I ventured to ask to come hither: I was tied to a tree, and the lash of his accursed whip, still writes the word *vengeance* across my shoulders . . . I'll *kill him*.[38]

The attack on slavery is particularly pronounced in the version by Shepherd and Creswick, simply entitled *Uncle Tom's Cabin* and performed at the Surrey on 27 October 1852. This, which initially is fairly faithful to the novel, was well received by the reviewers. To *The Era* it was 'the best adaptation as yet' and 'a decided "hit"'[39] and, according to the *Illustrated London News*, it 'achieved extraordinary success'.[40] Much of its dialogue is drawn from the novel – for example, none of the other adaptations give at such length the scene between George, on the run, and his former factory boss (not his owner), Mr Wilson. Wilson is a kind-hearted man, torn between his distress for George and his anxiety that George is 'setting [himself] in opposition to the laws of his country' and 'running such a dreadful risk'. In this version, as nowhere else, George details at length how his mother and sisters and brothers were all put up for sale:

> *George*: . . . She knelt down before this, my present master and begged him to buy her with me, that she might at last have one child with her, and he kicked her away with his heavy boot. I saw him do it, and the last I ever heard of my mother was her moans and screams, when I was tied to a horse's neck, to be carried off to his place.
> *Wilson*: I own these things are bad, but –[41]

George's refrain, that he owes no duty to laws that separate husband and wife and child, that 'crush us and keep us down' echoes one of the novel's constant themes.

That the continual reiteration of the attack on slavery is not accidental is evidenced by the way in which Shepherd and Creswick depart from the novel. For they conclude their adaptation with an out-and-out slave revolt on the Legree plantation, even as George is grappling with Legree:

> *Quimbo*: Oh Massas – The slaves are up, at the fall of the whip on Uncle Tom – they all now in mutiny 'cos they say he read 'em words of comfort. (Loud shout) . . .
> *Legree*: My pistols! sword! your gun! (Exit Quimbo) I'll teach em yet. (Re-enter Quimbo with others)
> *Quimbo*: Massa! Massa! They come this way (Enter slaves with lighted brands)
> *Omnes*: Down with the oppressor! (General fight – Legree desperate – he is beaten off)[42]

A satisfying conflagration and the (unlikely) arrest of Legree by Uncle Tom conclude the riot, though not before Tom has really acted the part of an uncle tom:

> *Tom*: . . . The mutiny no fault o' mine, no fault o' this poor chile's [i.e. Harry] . . . Oh don't hurt poor child – I won't run massa – I'll go back to the slaves, tell how bad to disobey the massa and rise agin 'em – told 'em so afore – when they wouldn't let me be flogged . . .[43]

Just as George's violent insistence on freedom is contained within his status as being of white and, in this version, aristocratic, parentage, so the satisfying spectacle of revolt is held in check by Tom's nauseating obedience. At the very end, the play harks back to the type of resolution familiar from the early nineteenth century (when the nation could begin to pride itself on abolishing the slave trade):

> *St Clair*: George, brother – my hand and [illegible] all are yours! What is your purpose?
> *George*: To breathe the air of Freedom's land, Canada! Where the roof that covers, however, humble, shall protect me . . . where wife – children, by sacred tie shall still be mine, and man have no power to sever those whom heaven binds . . . where waves the flag, nation's flag upon which the sun sets not, and wherever it waves man's right is held as sacred as his life.[44]

This was a constant refrain in dramas dealing with slavery, though Freedom's land was usually simply England.

Cassy – the female avenger

But if George can be seen in some of the plays as retaining some of the characteristics, in heroic rather than villainous mode, of the avenging black figure, Lemon and Taylor have, in their adaptation, gone some way further. For Cassy, the enslaved mistress of Legree in the novel, who is determined to revenge herself on him for her degradation, and is a figure who is usually dropped from the stage versions, is here given a central role. It is she who warns Eliza of (in this case) the sale of both her and her child to Legree; she who threatens and defies Legree; who attempts to protect Tom; who is only stopped from stabbing Legree by Tom and who, at the last, fires the fatal shot that kills him. Legree and his henchmen are pursuing George, Eliza, Cassy and Topsy up a rocky pass:

> *Cassy*: Stop; mind, George, Simon Legree's life is mine. It was his hand crushed me to what I am. It must be my hand that shall avenge me! . . .
> *Legree*: (*drawing his pistol*) Take that. Follow me! (*They rush to the rock . . . Cassy appears behind the breastwork.*)
> *Cassy*: Simon Legree, the hour of retribution has come. Die by my hand! (*She fires*)
> *Legree*: Curses on ye! (*He falls into the chasm . . .*)[45]

But before all this, Cassy has unflinchingly outlined her descent into degradation at Legree's hands to Eliza in a way that must have had the power to shock a contemporary audience. The sexual nature of Legree's transactions is quite explicit. Here he is, talking about Eliza, his latest purchase, to Tom Loker, in Cassy's presence:

> *Legree*: . . . that yellar gal – oh, brandy. Come, I'll wet the bargain. (*Cassy motions Tom to leave – he does so*) She's a beauty she is; quiet as a pigeon. Clar skin; eye-bright as lightnin', and teeth white as new dominers . . . (*sees Cassy*) . . . Cass yer! what do you look that way for?
> *Cassy*: (*placing her foot on the chair and resting her head upon her hand*) So you have bought some new hand, Simon Legree?
> *Legree*: Yes. What's that to you? I buy what I like and *sell* what I like . . . I'll bring home one as shall break your heart with jealousy, that's fact.[46]

His clumsy attempt to 'be friends' with Cassy and pull her on to his knee simply emphasises the point.

The detail of Cassy's stance – one foot on the chair, hand under her chin – suggests her power over him and is emblematic of her positioning outside the boundaries of respectable female society. That she was not white, that she was enslaved, that she was, nonetheless, contained within the strict overall confines of the melodramatic form made it, perhaps, more possible for the dramatists to push at the boundaries of what it was acceptable for a woman to express. She speaks graphically of being bought, sold and degraded; of being 'passed from hand to hand'.

Satisfyingly, Cassy does succeed in killing her man and, even more satisfyingly, is not punished by an early death either for her life of degradation or for the murder – again, surely a stretching of convention. She was not without peers on the stage – the month before Lemon and Taylor's drama was performed, *Sarah Blangi* (adapted from a French original) was playing at the Olympic. 'The conception of a creole having a slain father to avenge on a whole family, and pursuing her work in the spirit of Zanga and Iago forms the basis of a very powerful and exceedingly well-acted *drame*', declared the *Illustrated London News*.[48] Perhaps, though, the fact that Sarah was acting out of duty to her father, made her crimes more palatable. For there was no suggestion in the above review that Sarah was too strong a figure to take, as was, perhaps, implied in *The Era*'s mention of Cassy: 'Madame Celeste as Cassy, was, we cannot help saying, more melodramatic than natural'.[49]

Uncle Tom, Old Tom and anti-Tomism

Cassy apart, the thickly laid-on piety of the various Uncle Toms had already, by early 1853, begun to meet with a reaction. Some of this was simply due to the excess of plays which continued to crowd the stage, alongside all the books, pamphlets, novelties that were produced. The Sadler's Wells pantomime, for instance, moved swiftly from Uncle Tom to end 'with the exhibition of the greatest slave-master of all – 'Old Tom' (i.e., gin).[50] Fitzball's second version of Uncle Tom, at Drury Lane (introducing the character of a pedlar, specially devised for the travelling showman, George Wild) was pronounced a failure.[51] According to *The Era*, 'The subject is growing thin to barrenness, and the national sentiment is in a state of reaction from the tension into which it has been much too long kept'. Uncle Tom's sermonising 'might have been supplanted to advantage by the bones and banjo'[52] which, of course, shows how closely Tom plays – despite their overt message – fitted into a conception that 'black' equalled minstrelsy. The same mix was part of the Pavilion's pantomime, *Uncle Tom and Lucy Neal; or, Harlequin Liberty and Slavery*. This 'depicted the evil powers of slavery' but also included 'Mr. Cave . . . the celebrated delineator of nigger character, as Dandy Jim' winning 'immense applause in two very well-executed negro ditties'.[53]

By the Easter of 1853, Planché's extravaganza, *Mr Buckstone's Ascent of Parnassus* was winning favourable reviews. A parody of Albert Smith's *Ascent of Mont Blanc*, it portrayed Buckstone as an actor-manager, invoking the aid of Fashion and Fortune to discover what appealed to the public taste. And, along with the Corsican Brothers and other popular novelties, no less than six Uncle Toms make an appearance:

> *Mr. B*: Oh! my prophetic soul! my Uncle – Tom!
> But here are half a dozen uncles more!

> ... Mercy on us, with what fury
> Has this black fever raged! – The Olympic, Drury
> Adelphi, Marylebone, Victoria, Surrey!
> Against each other running hurry-scurry.
> Whipping their Topseys up in ways most scurvy,
> And turning the poor drama topsy-turvy![54]

'A clever little song' was then sung by Mrs Fitzwilliam, 'winding up with a wish most heartily responded to by the audience that [Uncle Tom] would go . . .'[55]

> Wherever you travel, wherever you go,
> Uncle Tom his black pole's [sic] sure to show . . .
> The stage had enough of Jim Crow,
> A jumping and a 'doing just so',
> And 'twould be quite a blessing if poor old Tom
> Would after that good nigger go.[56]

Some of the anti-Tom material, though, was far less good-humoured, cruder and more overtly racist than this. At the height of Tom-mania, for example, William Brough was responsible for two such burlesques, *Uncle Tom's Crib*, performed at the Strand and *Those Dear Blacks!*. The first piece, in which Uncle Tom is the landlord of a public house, revolves around the threadbare, Jim-Crow type situation of a romantic triangle in which Dandy Jim and Squashtop vie for the affections of Dinah. 'Meagre' was the epithet bestowed on it by *The Era*. Interestingly, however, its attack on Uncle Tom did not, at this stage, go down well with the audience:

> The attempts at some clap trap allusion to the prevailing mania about 'niggers' were by no means cordially received but . . . some hints at the humbug sentimentalism of the old womanry of Exeter Hall [symbol of evangelical Christianity] were smart and even warmly caught up.[57]

Those Dear Blacks, apparently based on 'French materials' sounds even more unpleasant. It is the story of a 'Yankee Nigger, ignorant as dirt and proud as Lucifer' who, coming into an inheritance and coming to England to find a white wife and white servant, is imposed upon by a penniless English clerk (played by Charles Mathews, the younger) and, as might be expected, ends up in his rightful place, as the servant. 'Mr. Suter makes a capital "darky", and is preposterous as can be, and ridiculous in the extreme.'[58]

When the *Westminster Review*, commenting on recent American literary production and a spate of pro-slavery novels, declared that 'Uncle-Tomism has had its day', it was both right and wrong.[59] The craze for Uncle Tom, though intense, was much more short-lived than that for Jim Crow. Yet, he was reprised on the stage only a few years later, when Beecher Stowe's next major novel of plantation life, *Dred* was also dramatised, in late 1856. And performances of Uncle Tom plays continued, sporadically, for a number of years.

But what he also left was his legacy of flattering, unresisting docility, piety and simple-mindedness to be added to the bizarre amalgam that was, by now, ready to be drawn upon for the representation of the black character on the stage.

References

1 *Athenaeum* (No. 566, 6 August 1836).
2 See Hazel Waters, '"An African's revenge": the black figure on the early nineteenth-century stage', *Race & Class* (Vol. 40, no.1, 1998), pp. 13–32.
3 See R. J. M. Blackett, *Building an Anti-Slavery Wall: Black Americans in the Atlantic abolitionist movement, 1830–1860* (Baton Rouge and London, Louisiana State University Press, 1983); Audrey A. Fisch, '"Negrophilism" and British nationalism: the spectacle of the black American abolitionist', *Victorian Review* (Vol. 19, no. 2, Winter 1993), pp. 20–47 and '"Repetitious accounts so piteous and harrowing": the ideological work of American slave narratives in England', *Journal of Victorian Culture* (Vol. 1, no.1, Spring 1996), pp. 16–34.
4 Blackett, ibid.
5 Ibid., p. 107.
6 *New York Express*, quoted in *The Anti-Slavery Standard* (1 July 1847), quoted in Fisch, '"Negrophilism" . . .', op. cit., p. 20. Also in Blackett.
7 See Howard Temperley, *British Anti-Slavery, 1833–1870* (London, Longman, 1972) and David Turley, *The Culture of English Anti-Slavery 1780–1860* (London, Routledge, 1991).
8 Harriet Beecher Stowe, *Uncle Tom's Cabin* (Oxford, OUP, 1998), edited by Jean Fagan Yellin. *Uncle Tom's Cabin* was initially serialised in *The National Era*, June 1851–April 1852, and published in two volumes in March 1852. The first, pirated editions appeared in England in July 1852.
9 See Harry Birdoff, *The World's Greatest Hit – Uncle Tom's Cabin* (New York, S. F. Vanni, 1947), chapter VII, 'Of the Tomitudes abroad', pp. 144–65.
10 E. Fitzball, *Thirty-five Years of a Dramatic Author's Life*, 2 vols (London, T. C. Newby, 1859), vol. 2, pp. 260–1.
11 Stowe's preface, op. cit., p. 3.
12 Mark Lemon and Tom Taylor, *Slave Life; or, Uncle Tom's Cabin*, first performed at the Theatre Royal, Adelphi, 29 November 1852 (Webster's Acting National Drama, vol. 17, no. 191).
13 *The Spectator* (No. 1275, 4 December 1852), pp. 1159–60.
14 *Uncle Tom's Cabin; or, the Negro Slave*, the Standard Theatre, 8 September 1852. British Library Addl. Mss. LC 52934C.
15 See Douglas A. Lorimer, *Colour, Class and the Victorians: English attitudes to the Negro in the mid-nineteenth century* (Leicester, Leicester University Press, 1978).
16 LC 52934C, op. cit.
17 Eliza Vincent, *Uncle Tom's Cabin; or, the Fugitive Slave!*, Victoria Theatre, 15 September 1852. British Library Addl. Mss. LC 52934F.
18 Ibid.
19 E. Fitzball, *Uncle Tom's Cabin*, Royal Olympic Theatre, 20 September 1852. British Library Addl. Mss. LC 52934g.
20 Ibid.

21 *The Era* (14 November 1852), p. 11.
22 Fitzball, Addl. Mss. LC 52934g, op. cit.
23 Ibid.
24 *The Spectator* (4 December 1852), op. cit.
25 Not that Lemon and Taylor thereby eschew the comic potential of the black; here the deficiency is supplied by a bizarre re-rendering of the character of Topsy, who is disguised as a boy and aids George in his escape, as his slave.
26 Addl. Mss. LC 52934c, op. cit.
27 Ibid.
28 '[W]hat the world sees as the curse of racial inferiority and cultural deprivation, *Uncle Tom's Cabin* views as the blessing of racial superiority and earthly trial. This Christian transvaluation enables Stowe to include the racist stereotypes of plantation fiction in her novel.' Jean Fagan Yellin, 'Introduction', *Uncle Tom's Cabin*, op. cit., p. xix.
29 Vincent, Addl. Mss. LC 52934f, op. cit.
30 G. H. George, *A Colour'd Commotion: an Ethiopian extravaganza*. British Library, Addl. Mss. LC 52934E.
31 See Birdoff, op. cit., pp. 152–3.
32 *The Spectator* (4 December 1852), op. cit.
33 *The Era* (5 December 1852), p. 10.
34 Shepherd and Creswick, *Uncle Tom's Cabin*, Royal Surrey Theatre, 27 October 1852. British Library Addl. Mss. LC 52934K.
35 *The Era* (5 December 1852), p. 10.
36 Lemon and Taylor, op. cit.
37 *Uncle Tom's Cabin; or, the Negro Slave*, Addl. Mss. LC 52934c, op. cit.
38 Fitzball, Addl. Mss. LC 52934g, op. cit.
39 *The Era* (7 November 1852), p. 10.
40 *Illustrated London News* (No. 588, 6 November 1852), p. 382.
41 Shepherd and Creswick, op. cit.
42 Ibid.
43 Ibid.
44 Ibid.
45 Lemon and Taylor, op. cit.
46 Ibid.
47 Ibid.
48 *Illustrated London News* (30 October 1852), pp. 354–5.
49 *The Era* (5 December 1852), p. 10.
50 *The Era* (2 January 1853), p. 10.
51 *Illustrated London News* (26 February 1853), p. 166.
52 *The Era* (2 January 1853), p. 10.
53 Ibid., p. 11.
54 J. R. Planché, *Mr. Buckstone's Ascent of Mount Parnassus*, Theatre Royal Haymarket, 28 March 1853. British Library 2304 D.14.
55 *The Era* (3 April 1853), p. 10.
56 Planché, op. cit.
57 *The Era* (24 October 1852), p. 10.
58 *The Era* (21 November 1852), p. 6.
59 *Westminster Review* (January 1853), p. 298.

BILL ROLSTON

'This is not a rebel song': the Irish conflict and popular music

The ability of popular music to link in with and advance popular progressive politics has, at times, been beyond doubt. Take Jamaica in
1978. Political violence between armed gangs loyal to prime minister
Michael Manley and opposition leader Edward Seaga was rife. Bob
Marley performed at a peace concert in Kingston where he brought
Manley and Seaga on stage. Standing between them and holding
their hands high, he and his group, the Wailers, sang 'One Love'. It
was, says Denselow, 'one of the great, strange moments of political
pop history'.[1]

   Twenty years later, Irish group U2 staged a concert in Belfast a few
days before the referendum held to ratify the Good Friday Agreement.
U2's lead singer, Bono Vox, brought on stage the leaders of two of the
main pro-Agreement parties, David Trimble of the Ulster Unionist
Party and John Hume of the Social Democratic and Labour Party.
Standing between them, he held their hands aloft and sang U2's
'One', followed by John Lennon's 'Give Peace a Chance' and Ben. E.
King's 'Stand By Me'.[2] The difference between Marley's gesture and
Bono's would have been even more stark if Bono's initial choice of
song had been accepted; incredibly, it was Rolf Harris's anodyne
'Two Little Boys'.

Bill Rolston is Professor of Sociology at the University of Ulster and the author of *Unfinished Business: state killings and the quest for truth* (Belfast, Beyond the Pale Publications,
2000).

Race & Class
Copyright © 2001 Institute of Race Relations
Vol. 42(3): 49–67 [0306-3968(200101)42:3; 49–67; 016113]

What could have been an act of homage turned out to be a case of pale mimicry. The Belfast concert was a government-sponsored public relations exercise, not the symbol of a truce between rivals. The audience consisted of young people invited by the two political parties involved, not representatives of the warring factions in the North, nor of the third main party to the Agreement, Sinn Féin.

The political power of reggae at a particular conjuncture in Jamaican history stands in stark contrast to the political subservience of pop at a key point in Irish history. The potential and limitations of pop thus revealed in this comparison form the focus of this article.

The limitations of popular music

In traditional sociological wisdom, the prognosis regarding popular music's ability to tackle political issues is poor. For Adorno in particular, and the Frankfurt School in general, popular music – like the rest of the 'culture industry' – suppresses and smothers political thought and cannot be progressive.[3] As Adorno concludes, all that popular music is capable of is the production of 'silly love songs'.

Such pessimism has dominated sections of left-wing analysis of pop music for half a century. Thus Harker dismisses pop music as pap for the masses produced by an industry hopelessly compromised by its incorporation into capitalist structures. The only exception to the rule is the space he affords to music which articulates progressive political aspirations and serves approved progressive causes – 'our' music as opposed to 'theirs', as he puts it.[4] One flaw at the heart of this argument is its over-reliance on the importance of lyrics: a song is political if it speaks of political issues.

The issue of lyrics in pop songs in general is problematic. There are those, such as Street, who argue that the meaning of music is forged in use, rather than emerging simply from the intentions of authors and producers. '[P]op's meaning is inevitably confusing',[5] and that is precisely its power; the listener attaches meaning and in doing so identifies with the music. On the other hand, Frith points out that 'most contemporary popular music takes the form of song', even dance music linked to recreational drug culture; the text may be minimalist and repetitive, but it exists.[6] Why are words so important? For a start, they power the central instrument in much of popular music – the voice. Moreover, music can give us words to express 'emotions that otherwise cannot be expressed without embarrassment or incoherence'.[7] At best, songs can work like poetry, providing an experience of transcendence beyond the banality of ordinary everyday living. When voice and words combine effectively, the emotion and passion – the poetry – is unmistakable.

This is relevant to the political potential of pop. Robinson, Buck and Cuthbert concluded in their global survey of musical meaning that '"political" music for most people, including the musicians we interviewed, is synonymous with politicized lyrics'.[8] In short, political songs have a preferred reading and are not open to endless interpretation.

That said, there is a second issue which needs to be considered, namely, pop's ability to speak for and to a community. For all that consumption is individualised, the magic of popular music is that it allows for *shared* pleasure. Yet, the 'community' that pop music can create is often fleeting: the imagined community of the individual fan, the temporary community of the audience, or the transitory community of the teenage rebel. Music's ability to create a sense of a more fundamental or lasting community is severely limited. But where such a community – based on shared interests of class, gender, race, ethnicity, subculture or age cohort, and so on – exists, there is no reason to believe that pop is unable to articulate, and thereby serve, the community's aspirations and needs. Street disagrees, his conclusion underlined by his use of dismissive adverbs.

> The record then simply provides a service, an excuse for the faithful to get together. It confirms, it does not convert . . . Where a song is used by a people already united by their politics, then it merely has to confirm their sense of unity.[9]

I would wish to question that conclusion. What Sivanandan imaginatively refers to as 'communities of resistance'[10] have mechanisms of solidarity and support; one of these has traditionally been music. There is no reason to believe that such a role is confined to ethnic or traditional folk music; pop music has the potential to inspire, mobilise and galvanise political groups. In this sense, music, including pop music, can be organic in the Gramscian sense of the term, growing out of a political constituency and speaking to and for that community.

In short, when preferred meaning, consumer interpretation and political community come together, pop music has the power to articulate and celebrate political aspirations and causes.

A brief history of Irish rock[11]

'In the beginning you had the showband and very little else.'[12] As rock began to emerge as a global industry in the 1960s, popular music in Ireland was dominated by hundreds of showbands playing cover versions of British and US hits. Their popularity was undeniable, as was their musical competence; Van Morrison began his musical career with the Monarchs, while Rory Gallagher played with the Fontana

Showband. Despite this, 'serious' musicians regarded the showbands as unoriginal.

At the same time, 'beat' music emerged in clubs in Dublin and around Belfast. Groups like Bluesville in Dublin and Them (with Van Morrison) in Belfast played American soul and R&B. When hippie-based psychedelic rock emerged, Ireland had its groups capable of producing the same sound, like Eire Apparent and Granny's Intentions. But they did not merely produce cover versions; the musical traffic was not one-way. Bluesville had a top ten hit in the US in 1965 ('You Turn Me On', Jerden Records). Them's 'Here Comes the Night' (Decca 1965) reached number three in the British hit parade. Skid Row toured in the US with the Grateful Dead. Thin Lizzy (Phil Lynott's group) made number six in the British singles charts in February 1972 with 'Whisky in the Jar' (Decca). And Rory Gallagher (of Taste) was considered in the same league as fellow rock guitarists Jimi Hendrix and Eric Clapton (see *Rory Gallagher*, Polydor 1971).

The success of the music outside Ireland – and not merely the aping of international musical trends – continued to be characteristic of Irish rock. 'Celtic rock' is a case in point. In the hands of a group like Horslips, it was an imaginative fusion of rock and Irish roots. Horslips' reworking of the eighth-century epic *Táin Bó Cuailgne* ('The Cattle Raid of Cooley') was an innovative masterpiece (*The Táin*, Oats 1973) and their *Book of Invasions* (DJM 1976) was an ambitious and relatively successful 'concept album'.

The sound of contemporaneous group Clannad was more ethereal than that of Horslips. In 1982, they reached number five in the British singles chart with 'Theme from Harry's Game' (RCA). It was the first time a group had sung in Irish on *Top of the Pops*. As Prendergast points out, they 'managed to transcend the limitations of the use of the Irish language by the sheer beauty of their sound'.[13] In fact, as Irish music of this kind joined the wider pantheon of 'world music', sound became all important. A prime case is that of Enya (originally a member of Clannad), whose ambient music merged the mystique of Ireland with the mysticism of 'new age' style (see *Watermark*, WEA 1988). Parallel with these developments was the growth of folk rock in Ireland. Artists such as Christy Moore, Donal Lunny, Andy Irvine and Paul Brady took a traditional music form made popular in the 1950s and 1960s by groups such as the Clancy Brothers and the Dubliners and transformed it. High points in this development were the groups Planxty and Moving Hearts. The latter's sound imaginatively stretched Irish folk in the direction of rock and jazz (see *Moving Hearts*, WEA 1981).

Ireland has also produced artists of global stature. Foremost among them has been Van Morrison whose music merges elements of rock, folk, jazz, soul and R&B. His constant search for identity through music has conferred on him the reputation of one of the most thoughtful of the world's rock singer/songwriters.

No Irish group has made more global impact than U2. Emerging from Dublin's punk scene in the late 1970s, by the mid-1980s, they had established themselves as the thoughtful, authentic voice of rock. Their overtly Christian messages and their more secular political ones have been rejected as inappropriate evangelism by some commentators, but, in the 1980s in particular, they managed to convey an aura of 'caring' which was commercially unbeatable; three consecutive albums reached number one in the British charts – *War* (Island 1983), *The Unforgettable Fire* (Island 1984) and *Joshua Tree* (Island 1987).

Part of the reason for the success of both Morrison and U2 was the marketability of their 'Irishness'. In Morrison's case, a constant introspective urge, which has led him to incorporate elements of Eastern mysticism, Jungian psychology and scientology in his music, took a distinctly Irish twist with songs such as 'Celtic Ray' (*Beautiful Vision*, Mercury 1982) and 'Dweller on the Threshold' (*Inarticulate Speech of the Heart*, Mercury 1983). As Bennett puts it, he 'reinvented himself as a Celt', eventually teaming up with the doyens of Irish traditional music, the Chieftains on the single 'I'll Tell me Ma' (Mercury 1988).[14] The popularity of many Irish artists is thus partly due to their ability to slot into a widespread definition of Irishness as mystical and spiritual.[15] No matter if the spirituality is judged to be overbearing, as in the case of U2, or eccentric, as in the case of Sinead O'Connor; Irish rock has found a niche in global culture.

It is difficult (and arguably unwise in market terms) for Irish groups to ignore their origins. Thus, the Corrs interweave Irish dance music in their easy-listening hits (for example, 'I Never Loved You Anyway', Atlantic 1997). B'Witched's 'C'est La Vie' (Epic 1998) ends with a lively Irish jig. Various Irish pop stars frequently include a version of the obligatory Irish traditional song in their repertoire; for Brian Kennedy it is 'Carrickfergus' (BMG Records 1996), and for Boyzone, 'She Moved Through the Fair' (Polydor 1996).

Even the most unlikely candidates for the label of Celtic mysticism, punk rockers, could not escape being marketable in part for their Irishness. In the North, punk had many of the same characteristics that it had in Britain, in particular, its badge of youth rebellion. The added dimension, however, was the conflict in the North. Although few punk groups made any direct comment on the political situation, all were viewed, especially outside Ireland, as breaking down sectarian barriers to bring young people together – a role seemingly at odds with punk's nihilistic reputation.

Punk in the South of Ireland was less angry. Perhaps for that reason it spawned a commercially successful 'punkish' group, the Boomtown

Rats, who produced a British number one hit with 'Rat Trap' (Ensign 1978). Lead singer Bob Geldof later became famous as the conscience behind Band Aid, a role arguably more in keeping with his perceived Irishness than his punk origins. A more orthodox Dublin punk group, the Radiators from Space, supplied one of the members – Phil Chevron – of one of the most successful punk bands of the era, the British-based Pogues. With songwriter and lead singer Shane McGowan, the Pogues invented 'folk punk', 'a schizophrenic style that could be at home with Irish traditionalism while insulting its back-wardness' (see *Rum, Sodomy and the Lash*, Stiff 1984).[16]

'The sound of silence': rock, pop and the 'troubles'

While these developments in rock music in Ireland were occurring, political conflict was rife in the North. Between the civil rights marches of the late 1960s and the peace process of the 1990s, the society wit-nessed intense warfare, sectarian assassination and intimidation and numerous human rights abuses. Over 3,600 people died and more than 40,000 were injured. To what extent was popular music able to relate to this violent conflict?

Music and politics have had a long and supportive relationship in Irish history. Nationalists and unionists have, during the last three centuries, had their own repertoires of songs celebrating their respective victories and defeats and articulating their aspirations. In the recent conflict in the North, both republicans and nationalists have been able to draw on some of these traditional songs, as well as producing new ones relating to contemporary events. Political song is thus a live and popular phenomenon; although there is little airplay on the official broadcasting outlets, the songs are performed in republican and loyalist clubs and are available on CD and tape.[17]

The situation is very different in relation to commercial rock and pop. Rock is said to be rooted in rebellion and freedom. It is imbued with the myth of authenticity; the singer means what s/he says and will never sell out to the culture industry. Rock is music with something to say. Pop, on the other hand, supposedly centres solely around pleasure, in particular the pleasure of romantic (usually heterosexual) love. Pop is inevitably commercial, its lyrics containing no deep 'message'. On closer scrutiny, the distinction is less watertight than first appears. The supposed authenticity of the rocker is often a thin veneer. Moreover, the 'message' of rock is often imprecise and indi-vidualistic; freedom is never defined, or is portrayed in individual rather than communal terms. Although artists like Sting and Bono have publicly supported groups such as Amnesty International, more often than not, when rock and sometimes pop artists turn to political themes or support political causes, they are making a personal statement. Mainstream commercial rock and pop do not sit easily with movements of resistance.

Consequently, few rock or pop artists have dared to touch the issue of the 'troubles' in the North of Ireland. Take Van Morrison as an example: 'While a large amount of his work wrestles with his very personal concepts of Celtic mysticism . . . troublesome aspects regarding his place of origin rarely, if ever, feature.'[18] On the other hand, some artists who have tackled the 'troubles' have easily confirmed the cynic's belief that pop and politics do not mix. A case in point is Boney M's 'Belfast' (House Records 1977); with its minimalist lyrics and catchy dance beat, this was the 'troubles' as disco.

Despite the relative paucity of pop songs about Northern Ireland, the phenomenon of 'lyrical drift' allowed for a broadening of the repertoire. Lyrical drift occurs when the meaning of a song is taken out of the context in which it was originally produced and reinterpreted by an audience in a different political context. This can be a case of political imagination (as in the use of Pink Floyd's 'Another Brick in the Wall' in apartheid South Africa) or political manipulation (as in Ronald Reagan's attempt to hijack Bruce Springsteen's 'Born in the USA' for the Republican Party cause). In the Irish case, there have been a number of examples. Labe Sifre's song about South Africa – 'Something Inside so Strong' – was adopted as a theme song by republicans in the aftermath of the 1994 cease-fire and was used effectively by Sinn Féin during an election broadcast for the new Northern Ireland Assembly in 1998. Tina Turner's 'Simply the Best' was used in the early to mid-1990s as a theme song by the Ulster Volunteer Force, particularly its mid-Ulster Brigade, and referred to the group's efficiency at assassinating nationalists. NWA's 'Fuck the Police' is popular with republican prisoners. The Boomtown Rats' 'Rat Trap' emerged as a popular song with INLA (Irish National Liberation Army) supporters after members of that organisation killed Billy Wright (leader of the Loyalist Volunteer Force, widely known as 'King Rat'), while he was in prison: 'It's a rat trap, Billy, and you've been caught.'

Some artists, however, did attempt to tackle the politics of the North directly. For example, Bananarama's 'Rough Justice' (Chrysalis 1983) relates in part the killing of one of the group's road crew, Thomas 'Kidso' Reilly, a 22-year-old from West Belfast, at the hands of the British army in August 1983. Their brief reference to the incident in the chorus – 'Innocent people passing by,/No time to run before they die./Don't call that justice' – was so oblique that it is doubtful if most listeners were aware of its significance.

In terms of the lyrics, the relatively few rock and pop songs which tackled Irish politics can be grouped according to one of four themes. First, Northern Ireland is an awful place, full of tanks, guns, hate and despair. Belfast-born rocker Gary Moore's 'Wild Frontier'

(10 Records 1987, the 'sole exception to [his] apparent distancing of himself from his native land'[19]) puts it this way:

I remember the city streets before the soldiers came.
Now armoured cars and barricades remind us of the shame.
Now we're drowning in a sea of blood, the victims we have seen.
You'll never hear them sing again the forty shades of green.

Elton John's 'Belfast' (Rocket 1995) is less strident, more questioning; but, even through the sympathy, comes a picture of Belfast as a living hell. 'In every inch of sadness, rocks and tanks/Go hand in hand with madness.'

The second theme is the desperate search for any signs of hope, no matter how flimsy. Take Police's 'Invisible Sun' (A&M 1981): 'There has to be an invisible sun,/It gives its heat to everyone.' For Simple Minds ('Belfast Child', Virgin 1989) the 'solution' is equally nebulous: 'Some say troubles abound, some day soon they're gonna pull the old town down./One day we'll return here when the Belfast child sings again.'

There is, of course, one source of hope: love can overcome all. This is the message of Spandau Ballet's 'Through the Barricades' (Columbia 1986).

Born on different sides of life, but we feel the same and feel all of this strife,
So come to me when I'm asleep and we'll cross the line and dance upon the streets.
And now I know what they're saying as the drums begin to fade,
And we made our love on wasteland and through the barricades.

A third theme involves condemnation of the protagonists. However, not all foes are equal. Specifically, loyalism's violence is invisible and goes without censure; condemnation is reserved for violent republicanism. The Cranberries' reference to a central date in republican history, 1916 in 'Zombie' (Island 1994) makes this clear: 'It's the same old theme since 1916./In your head, in your head they're still fighting.'

One of the most sophisticated songs of accusation was U2's 'Sunday Bloody Sunday' (Island 1983). To first appearances, this is surprising, given that the song referred in part to an incident in Derry in January 1972, when British paratroopers shot dead fourteen unarmed civilians during a civil rights march. U2 were undoubtedly aware of the potential reading of such a song as pro-republican, a possibility made more likely by the endorsement of Amnesty International carried on the cover of the album, *War*. Hence they were at pains to distance themselves from this reading. 'When they performed this song live, Bono always prefixed it with the introduction: "This is not a rebel song".'[20] Bono went on at later concerts to rip apart the Irish tricolour on stage, discarding the orange and the green so that he was left only with the white as a sign of peace. The first line of the song had originally been 'Don't talk to me about the rights of the IRA'.[21] Although it was changed to 'I can't believe the news today', Bono made sure that the song's preferred reading was decidedly anti-republican. After the IRA had blown up eleven people at a Remembrance Sunday commemoration in Enniskillen in 1987, Bono introduced the song in a US concert as follows:

> Let me tell you something. I've had enough of Irish Americans who haven't been back to their country in twenty or thirty years come up to me and talk about the resistance, the revolution back home and the glory of the revolution, the glory and dying for the revolution. Fuck the revolution! They don't talk about the glory of killing for the revolution. What's the glory in taking a man from his bed and gunning him down in front of his wife and his children? Where's the glory in that? Where's the glory in bombing a Remembrance Day parade of old-age pensioners, their medals taken out and polished up for the day? Where's the glory in that? To leave them dying or crippled for life or dead under the rubble of the revolution that the majority of people in my country don't want?[22]

Finally, tackling state violence has been the most difficult theme in popular songs about the Irish conflict. The most that some can muster is to ask demanding questions weakly, as in Paul McCartney's 'Give Ireland Back to the Irish' (EMI 1972): 'Great Britain you are tremendous and nobody knows like me/But really what are you doing in the land across the sea?'

Fellow Beatle John Lennon went much further in his *Sometime in New York City* (EMI 1972). This was his least commercially successful album, but also his most politically explicit. Two of the songs were about the Irish conflict. The first, 'Sunday Bloody Sunday', expressed naive, even embarrassing, sentiments. The other, 'The Luck of the Irish', worked better musically, its whimsical, almost folk-like, sound fitting well with the irony: 'Should you have the luck of the Irish,/ You'd wish you was English instead.' The song remains one of the very few pop songs to explicitly condemn the British state's role in the conflict in Ireland.

> Why the hell are the English there anyway?
> As they kill with God on their side!
> Blame it on the kids and the IRA!
> As the bastards commit genocide!

Despite the failings of the album, Lennon at least tackled the state head on. In doing so, he swam against the tide of what rock and pop had to say about the Irish conflict.

'Alternative Ulster'? Punk

As a musical genre, punk was a response to rock's decline into ostentation and commercialism. Punk was also a social statement which fitted the times. It provided a voice of protest in relation to unemployment, police harassment and youth alienation in the late 1970s and early 1980s. The rebellion was short-lived. The culture industry was able to absorb the challenge: 'Punk was a gesture, a fart in the face of authority – it was never an answer.'[23] But, while it lasted, punk was capable of delivering a strong political message in its music, articulating the frustrations of young people in Britain during a period of socio-economic decline. Although one section of punk, Oi!, was associated with skinheads and fascist movements, most punk groups took a more progressive political stance, in particular Rock Against Racism.

Given the ease with which British punk rebelled against the status quo in its lyrics, it was probably inevitable that the conflict in Ireland would become a theme, albeit a minor one, for British punk groups. Groups such as The Angelic Upstarts ('Last Night Another Soldier', EMI 1980) and The Pop Group ('Who Guards the Guards?', Rough Trade 1979), criticised British policy. The Au Pairs sang sarcastically about the strip-searching of women prisoners in Armagh Jail ('Torture', Human Records 1981): 'We don't torture./We're a civilized nation.'

However, the substance of punk's lyrics on the Irish conflict was sometimes much less radical than the form. Behind the noise and the rasping voices were songs such as the Gang of Four's 'Armalite Rifle' (Fast Product 1978), in its own way a simple peace song. 'It'll do you damage, do you harm./It'll blow your head off, it'll blow your guts out./I disapprove of it . . .'

On the other hand, the Pogues revealed that it was possible to pen hard-hitting political lyrics in relation to Ireland. Their 'Streets of Sorrow/Birmingham Six' (Pogue Mahone 1988), told the story of the miscarriage of justice against Irish people for the IRA bombings in Birmingham and Guildford in 1974.

> There were six men in Birmingham, in Guildford there's four
> That were picked up and tortured and framed by the law.
> And the filth got promotion but they're still doing time
> For being Irish in the wrong place and at the wrong time.

Finally, at least one Oi! band, Skrewdriver, laid down its marker on the North's conflict with perhaps the only punk song in support of militant loyalism ('Smash the IRA', White Noise 1983). Skrewdriver was led by National Front member Ian Stuart, whose influence on the development of right-wing punk cannot be underestimated. His prolific output of songwriting through the 1980s up until his death in 1993 served to forge a crucial link between right-wing extremist ideology and skinhead subculture. Music became the basis of a widespread neo-Nazi network in a way that more structured political organisation could not. There are currently estimated to be a hundred white power bands in over thirty countries, many of them trying to copy Skrewdriver's lead.[24]

Punk groups within Northern Ireland faced a different problem from their comrades in Britain.[25] For many young people who had grown up during the violent conflict in Northern Ireland, those who advocated, perpetrated and supported violence were as much a part of the establishment as the Thatcherite state was for British punks. The dilemma facing punk groups was whether or not to sing about the 'troubles'. The Undertones from Derry decided not to.[26]

The other option was to rage against all those groups that advocated violence; this was the approach of Stiff Little Fingers. Their targets included paramilitaries – 'They're nothing but blind fascists,/Brought up to hate and given lives to waste' ('Wasted Life', EMI 1979) and state forces 'Take a look where you're livin',/You've got the army on your street,/And the RUC dog of repression/Is barking at your feet' ('Alternative Ulster', EMI 1979). These were brave sentiments. But the belief that Stiff Little Fingers were harbingers of a new cross-community youth culture that would lead to an end of the conflict turned out to be somewhat premature. For all that they spoke to a large number of young people of the problems of living in a violent, repressive, morally stunted society, in the end their message was in many ways little more than a plea for some space for young people: 'They take away our freedom in the name of liberty./Why can't they all just clear off? Why can't they let us be?' ('Suspect Device', EMI 1979).

Such nebulous political thinking led to the decision of some punks, like Sean O'Neill, to espouse a more systematic political position. When his group the Undertones disbanded, he formed That Petrol Emotion, a group whose sympathies were unashamedly pro-republican (see for example, 'Big Decision', Polydor 1989). On the other side of the political see-saw, Paul Burgess's group Ruefrex set out to articulate the unionist case. In one song ('The Wild Colonial Boy', Kasper 1985), Ruefrex ridiculed Irish-American support for militant Irish republican-ism: 'It really gives me quite a thrill/To kill from far away.' Com-mercially speaking, That Petrol Emotion was relatively successful, more so than Ruefrex. But, in the end, it was the enthusiastic but ulti-mately non-threatening energy of Stiff Little Fingers and the even less threatening *joie de vivre* of the Undertones that were the lasting memory of Northern Ireland punk.

More than a decade later, the groups still clung tenaciously to their respective positions. In a radio series entitled *Rockin' the North*, broad-cast in 1994, most of the punk veterans interviewed stressed that punk's *raison d'être* was to escape from the 'troubles'. Most also rejected Stiff Little Fingers' attempt to swim against this tide. Stuart Baillie of *New Musical Express* summed up the argument:

> Without Stiff Little Fingers, bands like Rudi, Protex would probably have had an easier ride, because all of a sudden people were trying to get this 'rock against sectarianism' going. 'Rock against sectarianism' was a lot of people getting drunk in the Harp Bar; it was nothing to do with stupid, you know, 'I'm a suspect device: I'm gonna blow up in your face'. That was just nonsense. It was just tabloid songwriting. It was shameful.[27]

'Give peace a chance': folk songs

Folk music's connection with protest is time honoured. Moreover, folk can point to many instances where singer-songwriters were integrated fully into movements of resistance rather than simply making individual statements. Woody Guthrie articulated the Wobblies' politics in the US in the 1930s, as Ewan McColl did that of the Communist Party in Britain in the 1960s. In the US in the 1960s, folk rested easily with directly political themes such as black civil rights and anti-war movements. Yet, the problem for many folk artists was that their political acumen, honed in one era and society, did not easily transfer to other instances of political conflict.

Take the case of Joan Baez. In her opposition to the war in Vietnam, she argued that the US had no moral authority to wage war in Southeast Asia, that it should bring its troops home immediately, and that the Vietnamese people, including the Viet Cong, should be left to decide their own political future. She did not succumb to the state's anti-communist agenda. Translated to Ireland, this would have meant that she would have been opposed to British involvement, demanding the withdrawal of British troops and supporting the IRA's military campaign to unify the country; she would not have followed the state's anti-republican agenda. However, when Baez came to Belfast in 1977, it was in support of the Peace People. Formed in August 1976 in the aftermath of the horrific death of three children, the Peace People were quickly incorporated into a state and media offensive against republicanism. Baez's politics were consistent only at the level of form; in both the US and Belfast, she supported peace. But in one case only did she side with the anti-imperialist forces.

The dilemma facing Joan Baez also confronted indigenous folk singers in the North of Ireland. Some concluded that opposition to violence was paramount. In this vein, Tommy Sands effectively used pathos in 'There Were Roses' (Spring 1985), to condemn the actions of republican and loyalist paramilitary groups. The song tells the story of two friends from near the border, one murdered by republicans, the other in retaliation by loyalists. The moral is clear: 'An eye for an eye was all that filled their minds/And another eye for another eye till everyone is blind.'

Where Sands used pathos, Paul Brady employed irony. His mesmeric song 'The Island' (Fontana 1992) contrasts the miasma created by political violence with the bliss of 'making love to the sound of the ocean' on a deserted island. The song finishes in a masterpiece of irony:

> Now, I know us plain folks don't see all the story,
> And I know this peace and love's just copping out.
> And I guess these young boys dying in the ditches
> Is just what being free is all about.
> And how this twisted wreckage down on main street
> Will bring us all together in the end
> As we go marching down the road to freedom.

Ireland's most popular folk singer of the last three decades, Christy Moore, responded directly to Brady in one of his songs, 'The Other Side' (WEA 1987). The island of Ireland is portrayed not as an escapist paradise, but as a place where young republicans languish in prisons, where young people have to emigrate in search of work, where women flee secretly to England for abortions and where the violence of the British state is a fact of everyday life.[28]

Moore has been one of the few Irish folk singers willing to tackle the most politically controversial subjects, including opposition to nuclear power stations in the South.[29] Specifically in relation to the North, he sang about the blanket protest in Long Kesh prison, strip-searching of women prisoners in Armagh jail and the 1981 republican hunger strike. He also recorded two songs written by Bobby Sands, the first hunger striker to die ('I Wish I Was Back Home in Derry' and 'McIlhatton'), and was a central figure in the innovative folk-rock band, Moving Hearts.

In a situation where it became almost *de rigueur* for academics, poets, writers and others to preface their work with condemnations of violence, Moving Hearts' subject matter left them open to accusations of support for terrorism. Thus the *Hot Press* journalist Graham subjected the band members to an intense grilling on the grounds that part of one of their songs, Jack Warshaw's 'No Time for Love' (WEA 1982) could be interpreted as a call to people to help shelter gunmen and bombers.[30] 'The fish need the sea to survive, just like your comrades need you,/And the death squads can only get through to them if first they get through to you.' The band denied Graham's interpretation, but he remained unconvinced. He concluded that they needed to be more forceful in their rejection of this interpretation:

In Britain, neither the Clash nor the Beat have such problems and need not be subjected to what may appear over-pedantic questioning. But in Ireland, the gap between principles and armed policy is not so comfortingly wide.

As Graham implies, it was easier for artists from outside Ireland to write songs against state repression or in support of republican struggle. English folk singer-songwriter Maria Tolly's album *Voices* (Stroppy Cow 1986) contains a number of such songs. 'Living in a Nightmare' condemns the use of plastic bullets; 'Maghaberry Jail' is a call to feminists to support their sisters being strip-searched in prison and 'Troops Out' links the experience of the 1984 miners' strike to the struggle in Ireland. In a sense, the themes of Tolly's songs represent what Joan Baez would have been singing if she had been seeking exact equivalence with the songs she had sung in the US. But, in the absence of a widespread, popular, anti-war movement in Britain, Tolly's songs, while representing serious and worthy causes, were destined to be confined to a small, devoted niche market.

'Get up, stand up': reggae and rap

Reggae was, for a time, the cutting edge of political pop. It originated in Jamaica in the 1960s as a musical form closely associated with the Rastafarian religion. In the hands of a genius like Bob Marley, reggae was a powerful critique of capitalism and colonialism, though, in time, many other groups which adopted the reggae beat, in the process jettisoned the politics.

Rap's origins, however, are in the hip-hop subculture of black inner-city areas in the US. It thrives on a number of elements of African American youth street-culture: machismo, bravado, self-aggrandisement and the trading of insults. Themes covered include police brutality, gang wars, sexual conquests of women and attitudes (often negative) towards other ethnic groups. Consequently, leading rap groups such as Niggaz With Attitude and Public Enemy have been accused of racism, sexism, misogyny and incitement to hatred. At the core of the criticism is the question of meaning. Rap is a highly theatrical form of posturing and may demand no more identification with the lyrics from the performer than an actor has to the script of a violent movie.

No major international reggae or rap performers have tackled the topic of the Irish conflict. But both styles became incorporated in the repertoire of a number of groups which took a specific political stand in relation to the 'troubles'. House of Pain from Los Angeles is an orthodox rap group which just happens to be white and Irish. The content of their lyrics – numerous boasts about their powers of conquest over women, unspecified threats to those from different ethnic backgrounds who threaten their 'turf' and oblique references to police brutality – plus an overall macho style of delivery are clearly direct from the rap stable. For them, rap is the expression of ethnic identity and pride, as it is for disenfranchised blacks. As McGurk puts it: 'If it all seemed a bit like brawn over brain, with their centre of gravity in their groins, then at least the novelty value of white boys playing at being hard black men tilted the balance in their favour.'[31]

The critical question, however, was whether there was any political substance behind the macho veneer. Their reputation as 'republican rappers' seems to derive from statements they have made in interviews and attitudes they have expressed about the conflict in Ireland, none of which make their way into the lyrics of their songs. In McGurk's words:

Sadly, what could have been House of Pain's strongest and most interesting hand – their ideological adherence to a United Ireland in a music industry timorous of pop mixed with politics – is self-detonated by mindless sloganeering and trite trivialisation.[32]

Other groups incorporating rap and reggae styles, such as Black 47, Seanachie from New York and English-based Marxman, have had much more success at mixing pop and politics. Black 47 (named in memory of the worst year of the Great Irish Famine, 1847) used reggae to represent the struggle in the North as an anti-imperialist one; it was a case of the genre and the lyrics meshing neatly in an imaginative musical approach to the Irish conflict. 'You can break down my door, you can even strip search me,/Never gonna take away my human dignity./Beat me, shoot me, flame keep on burnin',/Never gonna put out the fire of freedom' ('Fire of Freedom', EMI 1993).

When Black 47 disbanded, one of the group, Chris Byrne, went on to form Seanachie (the Gaelic word for a storyteller or historian). The group produced the hard-hitting rap number 'Fenians' (1997), which recounts the involvement of Irish-Americans in the struggle for Irish freedom. 'Sedition's our tradition and it won't just go away./Say it loud, say it proud:/Unrepentant fenian bastard!'

As the name suggests, Marxman (made up of three young men, one of whom was the son of Donal Lunny of Moving Hearts) was an avowedly Marxist group. They used rap to put across a relatively sophisticated message linking contemporary experiences of miscarriages of justice against the Irish community to wider issues of colonialism ('Sad Affair', Phonogram 1993).

And my culture is as strong as a pyramid
And you will pay for these things you did,

Not just to we, but to the African,
The Asian and the true American.

There is no denying the popularity of these groups, albeit in a niche market, where they have managed to blend elements of popular and youth culture with local republican concerns. Black 47, Seanachie and Marxman have all played open-air concerts at the annual West Belfast Festival to capacity crowds. House of Pain was due to perform in 1994, but cancelled at the last minute. Seanachie's 'Fenians' was one of the most requested and most played songs on the local radio station serving the West Belfast Festival, Triple FM, in 1997. At the same time, those groups which have used rap and reggae to advocate Irish national liberation comprise an extremely minor element in the wider global world of pop music.

Conclusion

The relatively small number of songs about such a protracted conflict, along with the superficial treatment of the subject in a number of songs, would seem to confirm the impression that popular music is quite inept when it comes to such major political themes.[33] That said, there are variations in the ability of different musical genres to approach this political issue. Pop, as might have been expected, has been the most superficial, even naive. Rock, for all its claim to authenticity, has done little better; the politically articulate conflict in Ireland has not easily been incorporated into a genre which relates to more transitory, less articulate forms of rebellion. As a protest against rock and pop, punk was more amenable to political themes, but it is clear that punk groups outside Ireland found it easier to handle issues of state repression, armed struggle and so forth, than similar groups within the North of Ireland. Reggae and rap are genres born in the midst of black resistance and have therefore had some affinity to songs about Irish resistance; as a result, it is in these genres, as well as within folk, that the grander themes of imperialism and colonialism get what little airing there is in popular music about Ireland. That said, folk is split between those who have taken the base line of the genre – protest – as a signal to side with those who resist the state, and those for whom it is the inspiration to oppose violence, especially paramilitary violence.

Of course, the explanation of pop's relative failure to engage with political issues in this instance goes far beyond the limitations of particular musical genres. For a start, in the British context in particular, there is little incentive for popular music as a cultural expression to go against the stream of the common political views on the Irish conflict – namely, that Ireland is different and its troubles archaic, inexplicable, that the Irish conflict is about hate between people rather than the result of historical processes of repression, and that violence for political ends is never justifiable. Moreover, there were negative consequences for those who broke from the herd. Paul McCartney's 'Give Ireland Back to the Irish', mild as its sentiments may have been, was banned by the BBC. The Pogues' 'Streets of Sorrow/Birmingham Six' was banned under the broadcasting regulations in force in Britain between 1988 and 1994. The video accompanying the Police's 'Invisible Sun' proved problematic for the BBC's *Top of the Pops*, and so the song was pulled in September 1981.

Pop cannot escape the ties of ideology. For the popular artist, the dilemma, if any, is between authenticity and commercialism. Pop solves the dilemma easily: commercialism rules. Other artists, especially in rock and folk, believe that the musical genre allows them to make political statements. But these genres, no less than pop, are governed also by the ideology of individualism. It is rare for the 'authentic' statements of rock and folk artists to be grounded in communities of resistance. And, as individual statements, they are often born out of an ignorance, particularly outside of Ireland, about the nature of Irish politics. For those, whether outsiders or insiders, who can overcome that barrier, the issue of commercialism still looms large. At least one element explaining indigenous punk's remarkably tame political conclusions is the fact that groups played to young people from both sides of the political divide. While some bands, like Ruefrex and That Petrol Emotion, threw caution to the winds, few were foolish enough to cut off half a potential audience in advance. Even as politically committed an artist as Christy Moore was not immune to the demands of the audience; the repertoire of his concerts in republican West Belfast was noticeably more political than that of his concerts in the centre of town.

Music is now a major global industry and is restricted by the structures and ideological imperatives of that industry. As a consequence, most performers are far above the day-to-day political concerns and struggles of race and class. They are not organic to the communities of resistance which attempt to forge a collective, communal response to capitalism and racism; or, if they are, they are quickly incorporated into the music industry and its concerns. From within that virtual monolith, there are rigid limits on what they can say and how it can be said.

References

1 R. Denselow, *When the Music's Over: the story of political pop* (London, Faber & Faber, 1989), p. 133.
2 See S. O'Hagan, 'I was there helping to make history', *Observer*, review section (24 May 1998), pp. 2–3.

3 T. Adorno, 'On popular music', in S. Frith and A. Goodwin (eds), *On Record: rock, pop and the written word* (London, Routledge, 1990), pp. 301–14.
4 D. Harker, *One for the Money: politics and popular song* (London, Hutchinson, 1980), p. 87.
5 J. Street, *Rebel Rock: the politics of popular music* (Oxford, Blackwell, 1986), p. 7.
6 S. Frith, *Performing Rites: on the value of popular music* (Oxford, OUP, 1996), p. 158.
7 S. Frith, 'Towards an aesthetic of popular music', in R. Leppert and S. McClary (eds), *Music and Society: the politics of consumption* (Cambridge, CUP, 1987), p. 141.
8 D. Robinson, E. Buck and M. Cuthbert, *Music at the Margins: popular music and global cultural diversity* (London, Sage, 1991), p. 266.
9 Street, op. cit., pp. 80–1.
10 A. Sivanandan, 'All that melts into air is solid: the hokum of New Times', *Race & Class* (Vol. 31, no 3, 1989), pp. 1–30.
11 For a comprehensive and informative account, see M. Prendergast, *Irish Rock: roots, personalities, directions* (Dublin, O'Brien Press, 1987). More glossy but also informative is T. Clayton-Lea and R. Taylor, *Irish Rock* (Dublin, Gill and Macmillan, 1992).
12 Prendergast, op. cit., p. 11.
13 Ibid., p. 89.
14 R. Bennett, 'An Irish answer', *The Guardian* (16 July 1994). See also B. Hinton, *Celtic Crossroads: the art of Van Morrison* (London, Sanctuary, 1997).
15 The marketability of Irish music has been recognised by the government of the Republic; see Forte Task Force, *Access All Areas: Irish music – an international industry*. Report to the Minister of Arts, Culture and the Gaeltacht (Dublin, Stationery Office, 1996).
16 Prendergast, op. cit., p. 112.
17 For a consideration of loyalist songs, see B. Rolston, 'Music and politics in Ireland: the case of loyalism', in J. Harrington and E. Mitchell (eds), *Politics and Performance in Contemporary Northern Ireland* (Amherst, University of Massachusetts Press, 1999), pp. 29–56.
18 Clayton-Lea and Taylor, op. cit., p. 27.
19 Ibid., p. 28.
20 S. Goodman, *Burning Desire: the complete U2 story* (Chessington, Surrey, Castle Communications, 1993), p. 96.
21 N. Stokes, *Into the Heart: the stories behind every U2 song* (London, Omnibus Press, 1996), p. 38.
22 Cited in *The Food of Love and Hate*, part 3, 'Outside looking in', Radio Ulster (12 March 1995).
23 Graham Lock, *New Musical Express*, 1979; cited in G. McKay, *Senseless Acts of Beauty: cultures of resistance since the sixties* (London, Verso, 1996), p. 96.
24 See J. Cotter, 'Sounds of hate: the role of white power rock and roll in the development and diffusion of the neo-Nazi skinhead culture', paper presented to the International Studies Association, South, Annual Conference, Charlotte, North Carolina, 1998.
25 For a sympathetic celebration of punk's ability to transcend Northern Ireland's traditional fault lines, see John T. Davis's film, *Shellshock Rock* (Holywood Films, 1980). For brief accounts of each of Northern Ireland's punk groups, see G. Trelford and S. O'Neill, *It Makes You Want to Spit: punk in Ulster, '77–'82* (Belfast, the Punk Appreciation Society, 1998). In passing, it is worth noting that rave is currently viewed by some in a similar way to punk, namely, a musical form which brings young people together across the sectarian divide.
26 'It's Going to Happen' (EMI 1981) is possibly the only exception. According to Damien O'Neill of the Undertones: 'The original lyrics to this were about the

hunger strike . . . but the verses were shockingly cornball, so Michael wrote new lyrics.' From the sleeve notes of *The Best of the Undertones*, Castle Communications, 1993.

27 Cited in *Rock 'n the North*, part 3, 'Rock 'n a Hard Place', Radio Ulster (16 August 1994).

28 Paul Brady was seen to redeem himself partially in the eyes of republican critics as a result of his powerful song, 'Nothing But the Same Old Story' (Warner 1981), in which he practically screams his opposition to anti-Irish racism in Britain.

29 See F. Connolly (ed.), *The Christy Moore Songbook* (Dingle, Brandon, 1984).

30 B. Graham, 'Irish ways and Irish laws: the Moving Hearts interview', *Hot Press* (Vol. 5, no 21, 30 October–12 November 1981), pp. 7–9.

31 J. McGurk, 'Republican rappers cancel gig', *Irish News* (11 August 1994). House of Pain's first CD is entitled *Fine Malt Lyrics* (XL Recordings, 1992). See interview with House of Pain member Danny Boy O'Connor in B. Cross, *It's Not About a Salary: rap, race and resistance in Los Angeles* (London, Verso, 1993), pp. 249–52. Interestingly, House of Pain's CDs are often filed under 'Black music' in German outlets, a fact which would undoubtedly please the group!

32 Ibid.

33 An exhaustive list of pop songs tackling the Irish conflict would include: Black 47's 'Fanatic Heart' (EMI 1993) and 'Time to Go'; Luka Bloom's 'This is For Life' (Reprise 1990); Billy Bragg's 'My Youngest Son Came Home Today'; Billy Connolly's 'Sergeant, Where's Mine?' (Polydor); Phil Coulter's 'The Town I Loved So Well'; The Divine Comedy's 'Sunrise'; Everything But The Girl's 'Sean' (WEA 1985); Fun Boy Three's 'The More I See (The Less I Believe)' (Chrysalis 1982); Nanci Griffiths' 'It's a Hard Life Wherever You Go' (MCA 1989); Christy Moore's 'The Time has Come' and 'Unfinished Revolution' (WEA 1987); Sinead O'Connor's 'This is a Rebel Song'; Martin Okasili's 'Troubles Will Pass' (WEA 1997); Rogue Male's 'Belfast' (Music for Nations, 1986); The Rolling Stones' 'Blinded by Rainbows'; Ruefrex's 'Paid in Kind' (Kasper 1985) and 'On Kingsmill Road' (Flicknife); The Saw Doctors' 'Freedom Fighters'; The Screamin' Bin Lids' 'Running Up Hill' (1997); The Storm's 'Malice in Wonderland' (Silent Records, 1985); U2's 'Wake Up Dead Man' (Polygram 1997); and Andy White's 'Religious Persuasion' and 'The Walking Wounded' (Decca 1986).

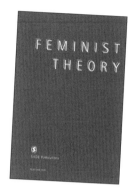

SEAN P. HIER

The forgotten architect: Cox, Wallerstein and world-system theory

Even if Wallerstein has so far given imperfect answers about the historical development of capitalism, still he has had the unparalleled boldness of vision to raise all the important issues . . . No book could have been more deserving of the Sorokin Award than The Modern World-System *– and no book is more worthy of continued attention and debate.*[1]

Given the recent expansion of world-system theory, it is surprising that so little attention has been given to the contributions of the late Oliver Cromwell Cox. A trilogy of volumes containing Cox's conceptualization of capitalism as a world system . . . predates by almost two decades most of the writing in this area . . . Oliver Cox deserves to be considered one of the founders of the world-system school of thought.[2]

In the 1940s, Oliver Cromwell Cox sketched out the parameters for his emerging conceptual framework, which explained capitalism as a world-wide socio-cultural system of resource exploitation, racial subjugation and international stratification. From his precursory discussion in *Caste, Class and Race*, Cox refined his theoretical conceptualisation of the capitalist world-system primarily in *The Foundations of Capitalism, Capitalism and American Leadership* and *Capitalism as a System*.[3] However, despite this early contribution to what came to be widely

Sean P. Hier is currently working towards a PhD in sociology at McMaster University, Ontario, Canada, and lectures in the Sociology Department at Brock University and the University of Guelph. [email: hiersp@mcmaster.ca]

Race & Class
Copyright © 2001 Institute of Race Relations
Vol. 42(3): 69–86 [0306-3968(200101)42:3; 69–86; 016114]

recognised in the 1970s as world-system theory, social historians, sociologists and anthropologists writing on the world-system have failed to deal with the founding work of Oliver Cox in any serious manner. In fact, the scholarly neglect of Oliver Cox has been so wide-spread that 'it is unsettling to learn that Cox is widely rejected in the "race relations" literature, his contributions are all but ignored in world-system theory and he is generally unrecognized in sociological circles'.[4]

In contrast to the sociological exclusion of Oliver Cox, Immanuel Wallerstein has made great strides in scholarly circles, to such an extent that the very name 'Immanuel Wallerstein' has become almost synonymous with the world-system approach. Establishing himself as a notable Africanist in the 1960s, Wallerstein's prominent position in American sociology was not achieved until the period following the publication of *The Modern World-System: capitalist agriculture and the origins of the European world economy in the sixteenth century*.[5] Since the appearance of *The Modern World-System*, three of a promised four volumes in Wallerstein's series have been completed, in addition to numerous articles and books dealing with various aspects of the world-system approach. Indeed, Wallerstein's scholarly reception has been exceptional, for, as Ragin and Chirot contend: 'Few American sociologists have succeeded in forming academic cults around themselves, and until recently none had ever done so through the writing of social history'.[6]

What factors have influenced the differential intellectual reception of Cox's and Wallerstein's writings on the world-system? Ideally, the answer to this question would rest on the principle of merit: that the ideas promoted by Wallerstein were methodologically more impressive and theoretically more sound than those offered by Cox. However, as I will show, the parallels between the writings of Cox and Wallerstein are striking and their overall theoretical and methodological frameworks are unmistakably congruent. It is somewhat curious, then, that Cox's ideas are not seriously dealt with in major volumes of world-system literature whereas Wallerstein's work has become a defining feature of the world-system approach.

My purpose is two-fold. First, to argue that Oliver Cox was the initial 'architect' of the world-system perspective and demonstrate how Cox designed a theoretical framework to explain capitalism as a system nearly twenty years prior to the appearance of Wallerstein's work on the topic.[7] Despite Cox's founding role, however, his contributions to understanding the world-system have been largely ignored and/or neglected. Therefore, as a corollary to this analysis, it will be necessary to look beyond the actual substance of Cox's and Wallerstein's work and examine the wider social, political and cultural factors which have served, at least in part, to draw Wallerstein into elite sectors of the academy, while simultaneously leaving Cox on the fringes of scholarship.

Oliver Cox

Who was Oliver Cox? Born in Trinidad in 1901, Cox embarked on a scholastic career in the United States which resulted in his obtaining a PhD from the University of Chicago in 1938. When Cox left Chicago, he held graduate degrees in economics and sociology. With such a background, it might be expected that Cox would be recruited by leading institutions. This was not the case. As was customary for black intellectuals in the 1940s, Cox was forced to seek employment at black colleges.[8] His first academic position consisted of teaching economics at Wiley College, Texas, as well as serving as the Director of the Bureau of Social Research. In his time at Wiley College (1938–44), Cox published at least eleven papers assessing the caste school of race relations, a critical line of thought which culminated in his first book, *Caste, Class and Race*.[9] But for reasons to do with his low salary and limited prospects for advancement, Cox left Wiley in 1944 for a position at Tuskegee University, Alabama.

In the five years that he spent at Tuskegee, Cox matured intellectually, earning a favourable, though modest, reputation for his many contributions (over twenty) to academic journals. Yet, up until this time, it is most probable that he remained relatively unknown to the wider intellectual community, as the majority of his articles appeared in the *Journal of Negro Education*. When *Caste, Class and Race* was published in 1948, Cox's popularity increased, but support for his work did not. Howard Becker, for instance, refused to write an introduction to the book because of its 'communist leanings', and Martin quotes William B. Selgby's response to the request: 'Dear Professor Cox, It's no use, I can't stomach the communist line.'[10] Cox had introduced a text which was highly critical of capitalism into a post-war socio-political climate, characterised by relative affluence and harmony. The economic prosperity brought on by the end of the war left Americans optimistic where their future was concerned, and sociological theory reflected this optimism in a functionalist mirror. Consequently, the kind of Marxist-inspired analysis that Cox had penned, centred on class conflict and racial exploitation, was met with either utter hostility or outright rejection.

In 1949, Cox abandoned his position at Tuskegee. At the time of his departure, Hunter and Abraham contend that 'his academic record was so impressive that he should have been able to obtain a position where ever he chose'.[11] Yet, on the contrary, Cox continued to face barriers to employment, never being granted the opportunity to teach outside of the South.[12] In the face of such resistance, Cox took a professorship at Lincoln University, Missouri, and it was at Lincoln that he wrote his trilogy on capitalism. Laying the foundation for what later came to be recognised as world-system theory, Cox's discussion of capitalism explores the origin, structure and development of capitalist societies and the larger system to which they correspond. But so unpopular were Cox's writings in the 1950s and 1960s that he was forced to pay $2,000 and $2,500, respectively, to have *The Foundations of Capitalism* and *Capitalism and American Leadership* published.[13] Oliver Cox died in 1974 at the age of 73.[14]

Immanuel Wallerstein

In contrast to the difficulties that Oliver Cox encountered in his professional career, Immanuel Wallerstein has reached a position in American scholarship that few sociologists aspire to. Born in New York in 1930, Wallerstein received his PhD from Columbia University in 1959 where he had begun teaching one year earlier. While his research interests were primarily centred on African politics for most of the 1960s, Wallerstein's early work did not diverge in any significant manner from the functionalist-oriented orthodoxy in developmental sociology. His first publication, *Africa: the politics of independence*, gave little indication that he was a budding radical. Nor did his second book, *Social Change: the colonial situation,* deviate in any notable fashion from functionalist theory – a fact which partly explains why Wallerstein's work was warmly received in modernisation circles. It was not until the appearance of *Africa: the politics of unity* that Wallerstein embraced a more critical sociological perspective, challenging modernisation theory by presenting imperialism in a dependency-style framework.[15]

In 1969, following the Columbia riots and the publication of *University in Turmoil: the politics of change*,[16] Wallerstein abandoned his tenured post at Columbia. After a brief stay at the Stanford Center for Advanced Study in the Behavioral Sciences (1970), he became professor of sociology at McGill University, Montreal (1971–4). It was at McGill that Wallerstein completed *The Modern World-System*. Outlining how the European capitalist world economy had developed in its modern form in the sixteenth century, *The Modern World-System* carried the argument that the capitalist world-system was characterised by an unequal international division of labour centred on economic and political exploitation. Wallerstein's arguments challenged much of the popular literature in the 1960s, and the intellectual reaction to *The Modern World-System* was mixed. On the one hand, scholars celebrated the appearance of the volume as a new conceptual break in social scientific understanding of capitalism, industrialism and national states. On the other hand Wallerstein, not unlike Cox, had taken on a critical project, challenging the orthodoxy in developmental sociology. It is important to realise, however, that, by the mid-1970s, when Wallerstein's Marxist-inspired world-system writings appeared, not only did he enjoy a favourable reputation based on his earlier work, but Marxism had also gained a certain degree of support in academic circles. To the young scholars who had studied at American universities during the 1960s, Wallerstein's writings offered an appealing alternative to the functionalist tradition in sociological theory in general, and developmental sociology in particular.

At the invitation of Terence Hopkins, Wallerstein moved to the State University of New York (SUNY) in 1975, where his reputation soared. Shortly after his arrival, he founded the Fernand Braudel Center for the study of Economies, Historical Systems and Civilizations, as well as the Center's journal, *Review*. In his twenty-four years at SUNY, Wallerstein has published a remarkable number of books and articles and has been visiting professor at no less than ten universities around the world, while numerous honours and awards have come his way. In addition to serving as the president of the International Sociological Association from 1994 to 1998, directeur d'études associées, Ecole des Hautes Etudes en Sciences Sociales (Paris) non-consecutively for several years and chair of the Gulbenkian Commission on the Restructuring of the Social Sciences (1993–5), Wallerstein has more recently (1998) been elected to the American Academy of Arts and Sciences. In retrospect, it seems to have been the establishment of the 'Political economy of the world-system' section of the American Sociological Association in 1980 which marked Wallerstein's canonical inauguration. Indeed, as Lentini observes, the creation of the Fernand Braudel Center and *Review* marked the beginning of the institutionalisation of the world-system approach to the study of social change.[17]

To summarise: in the 1950s and 1960s Oliver Cox produced a trilogy of volumes on capitalism, offering a conceptual model which conceived of capitalism as a stratified international system characterised by resource exploitation and racial subjugation. Yet so strong was the negative intellectual reaction to his first book, *Caste, Class and Race*, so dismissive and pejorative of Cox's scholarly reputation, that it resulted in the widespread neglect of his later work on the capitalist system. Not only were Cox's writings on the world-system ignored in the 1950s and 1960s, but contemporary world-system theorists have failed to deal with the founding work of Oliver Cox in any serious manner.

Discovering the world-system

When Immanuel Wallerstein published *The Modern World-System*, scholarly investigations of social history and historical capitalism assumed a new form. In a short period of time, modernisation theory lost credibility in intellectual circles, as Wallerstein emerged as the leading figure in world-system theory.

The appearance of Wallerstein's first volume on the world-system can be partially explained as a reaction to the positivistic intellectual legacy which theorised geographically dispersed, unequal socio-economic development in terms of differential levels of evolutionary progress. Observing that the industrial revolution was accompanied by a tendency to explain the growth of what came to be the modern world-system in terms of organic, progressive development, Wallerstein argued that the ahistorical models which had been constructed by classical figures such as Saint-Simon, Comte, Durkheim and Weber failed to understand or comprehend the social whole. Hence, he swiftly turned to Marx's oppositional doctrine for inspiration. But Marxism, too, was not capable of providing the methodological framework that Wallerstein sought. Unconvinced by Marx's discussion of stages of historical development, Wallerstein argued that 'the fundamental error of ahistorical social science (including ahistorical versions of Marxism) is to reify parts of the totality into such units and then to compare these reified structures'.[18] Essentially Wallerstein asserted that, in such a conceptualisation, nation states or national structures are erroneously presented as ideal types, reified into 'natural structures' of history and presented in nomothetic, positivistic models. Such an understanding, Wallerstein observed, is achieved a posteriori, not a priori. Consequently, the future can never be predicted.

Although Wallerstein's project can be seen as a reaction to the ideological legacy which conceived of the transition from 'traditional' to 'modern' societies as a process of natural progression (or evolution), a more immediate, closely related antecedent to *The Modern World-System* is found in modernisation theory, which became popular in the 1950s and 1960s. Influenced considerably by evolutionism and functionalism, modernisation theorists sought to explain the perceived inferior social, political and economic development of Third World nations as the result of a lesser degree of what was seen as an inevitable, unilinear progress. Paralleling the writings of classical thinkers such as Tonnies and Durkheim, modernisation theorists manipulated Weberian ideal-types, dichotomising societies in terms of 'tradition' and 'modernity'. In an effort to avoid 'the intellectual dead-end of ahistorical model building',[19] Wallerstein took as his unit of observation the social system.

To Wallerstein, the social system (or totality) has historically assumed two forms: mini-systems and world-systems. Whereas mini-systems refer to self-contained entities with an internal division of labour contained within a single cultural framework, social systems exhibit a division of labour characterised by an economic interdependency of sectors or areas within a larger system and are set within a multiple-cultural framework. Wallerstein argued, however, that there no longer exist any mini-systems in the world, declaring that the appropriate focus for analysis was the world-system. He identified two divisions of the world-system: world empires and world economies. Wallerstein defined a world empire as a social entity with a centralised political structure and a redistributive economic system. But the political centralisation of the world empire is at once its strength and weakness. Although it guarantees an economic flow from the periphery to the centre through taxation and tribute, the bureaucracy that arises in world empires absorbs too much of the profits, especially in times of social unrest and military expenditure. World economies, in contrast, are defined by Wallerstein as economic, not political, entities. Consequently, their linkages with external areas are based primarily on economic interests. And although Wallerstein argued that world economies have historically exhibited an unstable structure and become world empires, he asserted that, in the sixteenth century, the first stable world economy emerged: the modern European world economy.

Not unlike Wallerstein, Cox's disdain for traditional economic histories and nomothetic models of economic development led him to conceptualise capitalism as an integrated socio-economic matrix. While the intellectual traditions of economic history found in the work of Tawney and Weber, for example, were contributing factors to Cox's conceptual breakthrough, a more immediate antecedent to Cox's writings was the caste school of race relations.[20] From his preliminary discussion of the nature of capitalism in *Caste, Class and Race,* Cox placed considerable explanatory importance on the difference between caste and race relations, concluding that caste relations have to be distinguished from modern race relations.[21] In doing so, he engaged a wider study of capitalism, declaring that modern race relations are an exclusive feature of capitalism. As Cox believed that 'race prejudice' was a special creation of the ruling class under the capitalist mode of production, he argued that, by focusing on race in studies of modern race relations, scholarly observation hitherto had failed to grasp the true nature of race prejudice.

It was the principal shortcoming of orthodox sociological studies of race relations in the 1930s and 1940s, Cox asserted, that sociologists continued to take as their unit of analysis the single society or isolated unit. While Marxist models offered a greater degree of explanatory promise, Cox argued that Marx's fundamental shortcoming was that he was so consumed with class struggle in the capitalist nation state, he failed to realise the international character of capitalism. So, through identifying structural patterns in the world capitalist system as the appropriate level of abstraction for intellectual analyses, Cox outlined what he saw as the origin, structure and function of capitalism. For Cox, the capitalist system constituted a unified matrix of unequal social, political and economic relations. As such, 'capitalism' carried different meanings to different nations. At one extreme, it meant forced labour and racial humiliation; at the other, economic domination and resource exploitation. By concentrating analytical attention at the community level, Cox contended that the caste school had not only failed to understand the true nature of race prejudice, but the very nature of capitalism.

Therefore, rebelling against the orthodoxies of American sociology in the 1940s and 1960s respectively, both Cox and Wallerstein conceived of capitalism as a structural totality centred on outward geographic and/or economic expansion. Unique to capitalism, Cox and Wallerstein argued, was the formation of a unified world-system which encompassed not only capitalist but also non-capitalist societies, contained within one structural unit. Of primary importance to the system was the development of unequal economic and political relations concentrated along international lines. But before I explore the structure and function of the system from Cox's and Wallerstein's viewpoints, it will be useful briefly to examine their writings on the development of modern capitalism.

The development of modern capitalism

Just as Cox and Wallerstein are in conceptual agreement concerning the general nature of capitalism as a structural totality, so, too, they are in agreement on the developmental time-frame and general nature of modern capitalism. Where there seems to be some disagreement in their writings, however, is in their differential endorsement of the actual period when the capitalist system first emerged. In Wallerstein's opinion, the origins of the modern capitalist world economy are to be found in the structural peculiarities of sixteenth-century Europe. Building on the work of Fernand Braudel, Wallerstein identified 1450 to 1640 as the general time-frame when the capitalist mode of production appeared, growing primarily out of a 'linkage' between the Christian Mediterranean system, centred on the Northern Italian cities, and the Flanders-Hanseatic trade. Wallerstein argued that it was the failure of feudalism and the Hapsburg empire in the sixteenth century which enabled European 'agricultural capitalism' to flourish. Consequently, the capitalist world economy came to dominate

Europe as early as 1450, extinguishing any possibility of a resurrection of European feudalism.[22]

In a similar fashion to Wallerstein, Cox asserted that the solidification of commercial trade relationships in the Adriatic and Mediterranean facilitated the rise of the capitalist world-system. Cox devoted a considerable amount of space to detailing how the Italian city state of Venice prospered at the centre of this trade matrix, while the Hanseatic League controlled the trade of the Baltic region in the north. When looked at in conjunction with the expanding nature of the system, which was continually able to draw 'backward' areas of the world into its clutches, Cox held that the power of that system, and consequently of Venice, intensified as it spread across the globe. In this respect, therefore, Cox's discussion of the development of modern capitalism was highly similar to Wallerstein's. It was Wallerstein's belief that, from 1450, a geographically dispersed but highly complex division of labour developed across Europe and certain parts of the western hemisphere. Wallerstein argued that the newly emerging division of labour was contained within a single world market, in which economic actors produced agricultural products primarily for sale and profit. In turn, as the system continually developed, peripheral areas were drawn into the productive cycle(s) of the system at an increasing rate. But how did the system originate?

In Wallerstein's view, from about 1450, Europe was able to ascend into a capitalist world economy, not only because of externally oriented economic interests, but also because of a peculiar internal political formation of the state. Yet, despite the fact that, as he argued, the capitalist world economy appeared in Europe only after the fall of feudalism around 1450, Wallerstein made it clear that Europe was neither the first nor the only world economy. In the Middle Ages, city states such as Venice, Flanders and the Hanse had assumed a structural formation resembling a world economy; but, to Wallerstein, the 'medieval prelude' retracted after 1300 and failed to develop into a mature capitalist system.[23] It was Oliver Cox's belief, in contrast, that the very roots of the capitalist system could be traced to medieval Venice.

To Cox, Venice was somewhat of an oddity among the medieval city states. Not only did Venice enjoy a geographic vantage point at the estuaries of the Po, Adige and Brenta, but she was situated between the Lombard lords in Italy and the Roman empire at Constantinople in the east. As Venice was too far removed from Constantinople for the empire to exercise any serious constraint, Cox believed that the central factor leading to Venice's ascendancy to modern capitalism was her efficiency in the sea-bound trade of the Adriatic and Mediterranean. But Cox, like Wallerstein, was not so naive as to explain Venice's capitalist development independently of her internal social organisation. Not only was Venice characterised by a political, economic and governmental organisation geared towards capitalist initiatives, but 'religion [in Venice] was virtually inseparable from the philosophical and even from the scientific and economic thinking of people'.[24] It was, therefore, the fact that Venice was able to gain a stronghold in sea-based trade, coupled with her unique internal sociopolitical formation, that led Cox to conclude that medieval Venice represented the initial underpinnings of what came to be the modern capitalist world-system.

Despite their differential endorsement of the early underpinnings of the system, then, Cox's conceptualisation of the rise of modern capitalism is not too dissimilar from Wallerstein's. Although there appears to be some disagreement on the explanatory importance that each attributed to the early medieval city states, it is important to realise that Cox's interests in Venice were aimed at discovering the earliest structural formation of the modern capitalist system. Cox contended that capitalism emerged, not as a mature system, but as what Wallerstein identified as a world economy. By studying the earliest foundations of capitalism, he believed that the fundamental traits and the basic organisational design of the mature capitalist system could more readily be identified and understood. For Cox, it was not enough to focus analytic attention exclusively on 'mature' capitalism, as Wallerstein did, but, rather, in an effort to fully understand capitalism, Cox held that one must study the structural foundation of the system in its most rudimentary forms.

Cox's work on the development of modern capitalism, therefore, is similar to Wallerstein's in purpose and approach, if not in every detail. Both Cox and Wallerstein conceived of capitalism as a structural totality, independent of what they believed to be the repressive constraints of world empires. As such, both men placed considerable importance on the shared space of capitalism and feudalism. Wallerstein argued that agricultural capitalism emerged in the sixteenth century not only as the dominant but also as the exclusive mode of production in Europe. Cox, in contrast, believed that capitalism and feudalism co-existed, with medieval Venice emerging as a leader in the capitalist system, side by side with, but independent from, feudal empires in the east and west. Furthermore, both Cox and Wallerstein saw outward economic expansion as imperative to capitalist development. It was the strong, externally oriented economic interests of capitalist states, combined with a peculiar internal political formation, which led to uneven development within the system. This, in turn, led Cox and Wallerstein to devise highly similar conceptual models of the system. And, as I will show, the parallels between the geographical typologies that Cox and Wallerstein devised for explaining the capitalist world-system, and the dynamics they identified for the maintenance of that system, are virtually identical.

Structure and function of the system

What was the importance of Venice in the study of modern capitalism? In Cox's assessment, medieval Venice was part of an interdependent matrix that formed the structural foundation of the first capitalist system. This system corresponded to a hierarchical typology of capitalist cities: National, Dependent-Subject, Fairs, Kontors (staples) and Emporia.[25] First, National cities constituted the 'true home of capitalists'. As centres for capitalist organisation and activity, National cities flourished in commerce and trade. For the National city and its most advanced sovereign variant to develop, it had to be isolated from feudalism. This was seen first and foremost in Venice. Because organisations like the French and English cities remained dependent on, or subject to, feudal lords, their ascendancy to capitalism was delayed. 'The French and English cities, caught up in the stream of developing capitalism', Cox declared, 'remained relatively dependent and subject particularly because of the settled state of their feudal over-lordship.'[26] Fair towns, however, were essentially the locations of commerce and financial dealings. But they were dependent on National cities for their prosperity and thus were not initiators of capitalist commerce. Similarly, Kontors or staples were trading posts; but, unlike Fairs, they facilitated less sophisticated trade, primarily involving the collection and distribution of goods. And, finally, Cox differentiated Emporia (the most subordinated areas of the system) from Kontors, in that the former constituted the great markets or warehouses which were patronised by Nationals.

Cox believed that this early typology of the capitalist city represented the initial underpinnings of the capitalist system. Therefore, and significantly, Cox argued that capitalism first appeared not as a mature system but, rather, as a rudimentary form of modern capitalism, with Venice as its progenitor.[27] To function and grow as part of the system, however, several factors were vital to the prosperity of the capitalist society. Cox identified three: peculiar economic, governmental and religious structures. First, and most important, such a capitalist society is dependent upon an external network of commercial relationships. In this sense, the capitalist society is inconceivable in isolation from the capitalist system. Second, of central importance to the development of the capitalist society, is a government whose authority is not superior to the interests of the mercantile-industrial class.[28] The governmental structure has to facilitate the demands of individual capitalists. And third, dating back to the origins of capitalism in Venice, there has been an inherent conflict in the capitalist society between the church and the city.[29] For the capitalist society to prosper, the church must be under the control of the state. With these three factors present, Cox argued, the capitalist society can be differentiated from previous structural organisations.

In a similar vein to Cox, Wallerstein conceived of the capitalist world-system as a single economic unit, unequally stratified along geographic lines. But, to a considerably greater extent than Cox, Wallerstein emphasised the political disunity of the system, which he believed enabled individual entrepreneurs to prosper economically from the direct and conscious exploitation of peripheral areas, their resources and labour power. The nature of this exploitative relationship served to deepen social fractures between core and peripheral areas of the system, simultaneously strengthening and weakening the economic and political power of core and peripheral nations, respectively. However, although Cox did not explicitly place as much explanatory importance on the political autonomy of the nation state, it would be incorrect to conclude that Wallerstein's conceptualisation diverges in any clear-cut fashion from Cox's. For Cox outlined several internal features of capitalist societies that he believed were necessary for successful participation in the wider system. Indeed, it was Venice's uniquely isolated political structure, combined with her externally oriented economic interests, which facilitated her ascendancy to a dominating position in the capitalist system.

To Wallerstein, the division of labour that emerged along geographically stratified lines in Europe in the sixteenth century was comprised of three identifiable zones: cores, peripheries and semi-peripheries. Through a series of historical, geographical and ecological 'accidents' in the sixteenth century, agricultural production in north-western Europe, argued Wallerstein, developed at a more accelerated rate than in other areas of Europe. In turn, these 'core' areas came to favour tenancy and wage labour as the primary mechanisms of labour control. Conversely, eastern Europe and the western hemisphere emerged as peripheral areas in the world economy, specialising in a variety of export products. The nature of the core-periphery relationship was characterised by the exploitation of the periphery by core states. But the core-periphery distinction in Wallerstein's model is more accurately conceived of as a continuum (rather than as two ideal-typical structural units) with the semi-peripheries falling somewhere between the extremes. Around 1640, Mediterranean Europe emerged as a semi-periphery in the world economy, centred on sharecropping and the production of industrial products. For Wallerstein, the three primary areas of the system had become consolidated by 1640, forming the structural foundation of the capitalist world economy.

Up to this point, it is clear that both Cox and Wallerstein viewed capitalism as a stratified world-system. Whereas Wallerstein argued that 'agricultural capitalism' emerged in north-western Europe in the sixteenth century, Cox traced the structural foundation of capitalism to medieval Venice. It is important to realise, however, that Cox's writings were by no means confined to 'early capitalism'. It was Cox's belief that the capitalist system had become irreversibly orga- nised around the beginning of the thirteenth century and reached its highest state of perfection between 1870 and 1914. He argued that the nature of the system, from its early underpinnings in Venice, remained relatively stable. When Great Britain assumed leadership of the system, a constant struggle ensued with the United States and Germany for international market domination. And it was the solidifi- cation of geographical divisions in the world-system, coupled with growing transnational inequalities, which motivated Cox to refine his structural typology of the capitalist city in *Capitalism as a System.* Outlining five structural gradients of the capitalist system – Leaders, Subsidiaries, Progressives, Dependents and Passives – Cox argued that this structural formation of the system corresponded to the early formation of the capitalist city. By studying the early formation of the system, Cox believed that it could more readily be understood.

Hence, Cox's typology of the early capitalist society, and his subsequent typology of the capitalist system, are remarkably similar to Wallerstein's. While they seem to diverge on their endorsement of the period in which capitalism emerged, the importance of this distinc- tion tends to rest on whether attention is centred on 'early' or 'mature' capitalism. Although Wallerstein asserted that capitalism did not emerge until after the decline of feudalism and the Hapsburg empire, it is obvious from Cox's typology of the capitalist system that he was focusing on roughly the same period of time. And, while their writings are presented as conceptual counter-currents to orthodox 'deductivist' schools of thought, neither writer was able to escape deductive analysis. It is overwhelmingly clear from Wallerstein's final chapter of *The Modern World-System*, 'Theoretical reprise', and Cox's final volume, *Capitalism as a System*, that they are both operating according to pre- conceived models. Nonetheless, Cox and Wallerstein came out of a radical tradition in the sense that they both rebelled against orthodox schools of thought, and they can both be credited with devising a counter-blast to mainstream sociology. Given the remarkable parallels between the models offered by Cox and Wallerstein, it is surprising that Cox is not ranked among the key founders in world-system theory.

The forgotten architect

Almost twenty years have passed since Herbert M. Hunter initiated what came to be a sequence of largely unsuccessful attempts to draw serious attention to the sociology of Oliver Cox.[30] In light of the special issue of *Research in Race and Ethnic Relations* (1997) on *The Black Intellectuals*, which granted Cox a modest degree of attention, and, more importantly, the recent edition of *Research in Race and Ethnic Relations*, entitled *The Life and Work of Oliver C. Cox: new perspectives*, the time is fitting to revisit Oliver Cox's sociological vision. I can think of no better way to approach this than by reinforcing Cox's rightful place in the founding circles of world-system theory.

Both Cox's and Wallerstein's writings on the world-system can be explained, at least in part, as conceptual reactions to diverse strands of functionalism and positivism. Yet it was not until the publication of Wallerstein's *The Modern World-System* that the study of social history and historical capitalism gained widespread popularity in sociology. Certainly, discussions of historical capitalism appeared in the works of Polanyi and Dobb, as well as in Weber's much less recognised discussion of the institutional aspects of western capitalism in *General Economic History*.[31] But the appeal of historical analyses of world capitalism in general, and Marxist-inspired writings in particular, has only substantially increased in the past two decades. How can the staggering success of Wallerstein's world-system theory be explained in the light of Oliver Cox's scholarly exclusion?

Fundamentally, both Cox and Wallerstein can be seen as intellectual radicals. Whereas Cox launched numerous attacks against individual scholars and schools of thought alike, Wallerstein singled out orthodox traditions for critical evaluation. But Wallerstein's break from orthodoxy led him to a professional location far removed from the position that Oliver Cox found himself in. Perhaps one of the most glaring differences between Cox and Wallerstein is that Cox was a black scholar in a white-dominated intellectual environment. However, as I have commented elsewhere, the fact that Cox was black does not entirely explain his marginalisation, although it is of central importance.[32] To be sure, black intellectuals in the 1940s and 1950s faced many barriers, but black scholars such as Charles S. Johnson, E. Franklin Frazier and Allison Davis made great strides in both black and white scholarly circles.[33] It is important to realise that Cox attracted no greater attention from leading black institutions such as Howard, Fisk and Atlanta than he did from any other (white) American university.

Equally revealing of the underlying factors contributing to Cox's exclusion is his relationship to Marxism. While a certain degree of controversy has surrounded the tendency to label as Marxist either Oliver Cox or his writings,[34] there is little debate concerning the fact that Cox was ignored after 1948 because he was perceived as a loyal adherent of Marx. Considering that Cox advocated the eradication of capitalism in favour of a democratic society free of class stratification, it is little wonder that his early work was rejected by its postwar American audience. The intellectual and political climate of the late 1940s and early 1950s was hostile to any deviation from post-war economic triumphalism; orthodoxies not only went unquestioned but were not to be questioned – this was, after all, a period that led to McCarthyism. The rigidity of race barriers was matched by the rigidity of intellectual barriers. Cox attempted to breach both. Yet, some twenty years later, in a near identical manner to Cox, Wallerstein advocated the same fundamental position and acknowledged the 'monumental' role that Karl Marx had played in political history:

> Socialism involves the creation of a new kind of *world*-system, neither a redistributive world-empire nor a capitalist world-economy but a socialist world-government. I don't see this projection as being in the least utopian but I also don't feel its institution is imminent. It will be the outcome of a long struggle in forms that may be familiar and perhaps in very new forms that will take place in *all* the areas of the world-economy (Mao's continual 'class struggle').[35]

Although Wallerstein rejected the 'mechanics' of Marx's theory of the proletarian revolution, he did not dismiss Marx's general vision. Like so many other scholars in the late 1960s and early 1970s, Wallerstein believed that the working-class revolution had not transpired in the way that Marx predicted, in part because the proletariat was concentrated in peripheral areas of the world economy – the 'Third World'. Offering an alternative to Marx's predictive failure, therefore, Wallerstein argued that the only revolution in the world economy capable of leading to a successful socialist system was revolution on a world scale. For a successful transition to socialism, Wallerstein believed that the entire world-system had to be revolutionised. To those scholars in the mid-1970s who were sympathetic to the general Marxist position, Wallerstein offered an attractive alternative to the failures of Marx's original prediction.

To be sure, neither Cox nor Wallerstein were dogmatically faithful to the teachings of Karl Marx, and they both acknowledged that Marx was useful only to a certain extent. Cox realised this early on when he wrote that:

> Marxist hypotheses are 'servants, not masters' . . . it has been said that Karl Marx himself was not a Marxist because in his studies he strived to understand modern society, while religious Marxists, in their exegetical discussions, centered their attention not upon the ongoing social system but rather on explanation and criticism of Marx.[36]

Yet, regardless of Cox's insight, neither the social nor the intellectual climate of the 1950s was at all conducive to the kind of Marxist-inspired analysis that he had written. By the time that *The Modern World-System* was published in 1974, however, Marxism had gained a certain degree of intellectual respect. Modernisation theory had endured considerable criticism throughout the latter 1960s and functionalism as the dominant sociological perspective was losing support. Essentially, the reason that Wallerstein was able to bridge the gap between Marx's scholarly appeal and the failures of Marx's revolutionary predictions, was that his work 'fitted' the intellectual temperament of the 1970s. While Oliver Cox stands as the initial architect of the world-system perspective, Immanuel Wallerstein remains its senior developer.

References

1 Theda Skocpol, 'Wallerstein's world-capitalist system: a theoretical and historical critique', *American Journal of Sociology* (Vol. 82, no. 5, 1977), p. 1089.
2 Herbert Hunter, 'The world-system theory of Oliver C. Cox', *Monthly Review* (October 1985), pp. 44, 54.
3 Oliver C. Cox, *The Foundations of Capitalism* (London, Peter Owen, 1959); *Capitalism and American Leadership* (New York, Philosophical Library, 1962); *Capitalism as a System* (New York, Monthly Review Press, 1964).
4 Sean P. Hier, 'Structures of orthodoxy and the sociological exclusion of Oliver Cox', *Research in Race and Ethnic Relations* (Vol. 11, 2000), p. 304.
5 Immanuel Wallerstein, *The Modern World-System: capitalist agriculture and the origins of the European world economy in the sixteenth century* (Cambridge, CUP, 1974). See also Immanuel Wallerstein, 'The rise and future demise of the world capitalist system: concepts for comparative analysis', *Comparative Studies in Society and History* (Vol. 16, 1974), pp. 387–415.
6 Theda Skocpol (ed.), *Vision and Method in Historical Sociology* (Cambridge, Cambridge University Press, 1984), p. 276.
7 Neither Cox nor Wallerstein were by any means the first writers to discuss the international nature of capitalism. Marx, for example, in his final chapter of *Capital* (Vol. I, Chapter 33, p. 931), opened his discussion of 'The modern theory of colonization' with the declaration that: 'Political economy confuses, in principle, two different kinds of private property, one of which rests on the labour of the producer himself, and the other on the exploitation of the labour of others . . . Where the capitalist has behind him the power of the mother country, he tries to use force to clear out of the way the modes of production and appropriation which rest on the personal labour of the independent producer.' Nonetheless, although Marx realised the fundamental nature of colonial labour expropriation, Cox's and Wallerstein's writings on the capitalist system represent systematic attempts to formulate a specific theory of international capitalism.
8 Herbert Hunter and Sameer Abraham, *Race, Class and the World System* (New York, Monthly Review Press, 1987).
9 Although Cox had completed *Caste, Class and Race* while he was at Wiley, possibly earning for himself the reputation of a black scholar trying to publish a Marxist text, he was not able to publish the book until the late 1940s.
10 Elmer P. Martin, *The Sociology of Oliver C. Cox: a systematic inquiry* (University of Atlanta, MA thesis, 1971), p. 22.
11 *Race, Class and the World System*, op. cit., p. xxvii.
12 It is important to realise that Cox was attracting no more support from leading black intellectuals such as Charles S. Johnson and E. Franklin Frazier at Fisk and Howard, respectively, than he was from the larger white institutions. Like Cox, Frazier and Johnson had received their graduate training from Chicago but

neither Johnson nor Frazier endorsed the critical, anti-orthodox position that Cox promoted. Johnson and Frazier, like their Chicago teachers, promoted a value-neutral sociology, not conducive to the critical social theory promoted by Cox. Given the fact that Cox had singled out leading sociological figures at Chicago, such as Robert Park, in *Caste, Class and Race* for critical evaluation, it should be of little surprise that support from Johnson and Frazier was not forthcoming.

13 *The Sociology of Oliver C. Cox: a systematic inquiry*, op. cit.

14 Following his retirement from Lincoln in 1970, Cox became Distinguished Professor of Sociology at Wayne State University, Detroit, at the invitation of Alvin W. Rose. In the three years that he spent at Wayne State, he was able to complete *Race Relations: elements and dynamics*, published posthumously in 1976.

15 Immanuel Wallerstein, *Africa: the politics of independence* (New York, Vintage Books, 1961); *Social Change: the colonial situation* (New York, Wiley, 1966); *Africa: the politics of unity* (New York, Random House, 1967).

16 Immanuel Wallerstein, *University in Turmoil: the politics of change* (New York, Atheneum, 1969).

17 Orlando Lentini, 'Immanuel Wallerstein', *International Sociology* (Vol. 13, no. 1, 1998), pp. 135–9.

18 Immanuel Wallerstein, 'The rise and future demise of the world capitalist system: concepts for comparative analysis', *Comparative Studies in Society and History* (Vol. 16), p. 389.

19 Ibid., p. 388.

20 The caste school of race relations held that the American South was characterised by a split-stratification system whereby a social barrier divided the black and white 'races' into distinct castes. Not only did its proponents conceive of a caste system stratified along racial lines, but argued that, within each caste, there existed a stratified class system. The caste school argued that class movement/mobility within castes was socially permitted, but inter-caste mobility was socially restricted.

21 Cox argued that, while race is a closed system, the same could not be said for caste. Directing attention to the Hindu caste system, Cox asserted not only that the Hindu system had never been based on skin colour or blood relations, but that, unlike the southern United States, the Hindu system could not be characterised by conflict.

22 Wallerstein believed that it was the fundamental shortcoming of the Marxist distinction between merchant and industrial capitalism that led many observers to question the label of 'capitalist' for any structural organisation prior to the industrial revolution in England. On the contrary, argued Wallerstein, despite the debate over the degree of proletarianisation of labour power or the centralisation of production prior to the eighteenth century, the ultimate fallacy of this type of thinking is to place too great an emphasis on the specific characteristics of wage labour. Hence, he proceeded to draw attention to the unique nature of commodified labour power in the sixteenth century, which he believed was significantly different from the relationship of a feudal serf to his lord in eleventh-century Burgundy, where the economy was not oriented to a world market and where labour power was neither bought nor sold. Indeed, serfs in Poland or encomienda in New Spain, Wallerstein claimed, were in fact 'paid' for cash cropping in the sixteenth century in a manner different from, but inherently related to, wage labour under 'industrial capitalism'.

23 *The Modern World-System: capitalist agriculture and the origins of the European world economy in the sixteenth century*, op. cit., pp. 15–49.

24 *The Foundations of Capitalism*, op. cit., p. 57.

25 Ibid., pp. 25–8.

26 Ibid., p. 27.

27 Ibid., pp. 30–139.

28 *Capitalism as a system*, op. cit., p. 19.

29 The central feature of the religious establishment in Venice was that it was under the control of the state. Cox argued that religion was virtually inseparable from the philosophical, scientific and economic thinking of the people. He believed that it was never economically sound for religion to be repressed by the state and argued that, while religious freedom was everywhere highly restricted, Venice had early on discovered the utility of tolerance.
30 Herbert M. Hunter, *The Life and Work of Oliver C. Cox* (University of Boston, PhD Thesis, 1981); 'Oliver C. Cox: a biographical sketch of his life and work', *Phylon* (Vol. 44, no. 14, 1983), pp. 249–61; 'Oliver C. Cox: Marxist or intellectual radical?', *Journal of the History of Sociology* (Vol. 11, no. 5, 1983), pp.1–27; 'The world-system theory of Oliver C. Cox', *Monthly Review* (October, 1986), pp. 43–53; 'The political economic thought of Oliver C. Cox', in Thomas Boston's *A Different Vision: African American economic thought* (New York, Routledge, 1996); *Race Class and the World System*, op cit.; 'The sociology of Oliver C. Cox: new perspectives' (ed.), *Research in Race and Ethnic Relations* (Vol. 11, 2000).
31 Karl Polanyi, *The Great Transformation: the political and economic origins of our time* (New York, Rinehart, 1944); Maurice Dobbs, *Studies in the Development of Capitalism* (New York, International, 1963).
32 'Structures of orthodoxy and the sociological exclusion of Oliver Cox', op. cit.
33 After completing his PhD at Chicago, Frazier held a professorship at Fisk from 1929 to 1934 before assuming the position of head of sociology at Howard in 1934 and the presidency of the American Sociological Society (now the American Sociological Association) in 1948. Johnson graduated with his doctorate from Chicago as well, going on to become president of Fisk University in 1949. And Allison Davis became widely recognised when he published *Deep South* under the leadership of W. Lloyd Warner, with Mary and Burleigh Gartner in 1941.
34 Robert Miles, 'Class, race and ethnicity: a critique of Cox's theory', *Ethnic and Racial Studies* (Vol. 3, no. 2, 1980), pp. 169–87; Herbert Hunter, 'Oliver C. Cox: marxist or intellectual radical?', *Journal of the History of Sociology* (Vol. 11, no. 5, 1983), pp. 1–27.
35 'The rise and future demise of the world capitalist system: concepts for comparative analysis', op. cit., p. 415.
36 *Caste, Class and Race*, op. cit., p. xi.

Commentary

UK

Refugees from globalism*

As the Immigration and Asylum Act begins to bite in Britain, and the government is forced to justify its inhuman treatment of asylum seekers, the Campaign Against Racism and Fascism asked A. Sivanandan for his overview and analysis.

The distinction between political refugees and economic migrants is a bogus one, susceptible to different interpretations by different interests at different times. The UK is quite happy to take in economic migrants if they are businessmen (with the requisite £250,000), professionals, or technologically skilled. It needs highly skilled people, preferably ready-made. It welcomes the computer wizards of 'silicon valley' of Bangalore but does not want the persecuted peoples of Sri Lanka or the Punjab. And it is these it terms economic migrants – with all its connotations of scrounging and begging.

From industrial to global capitalism
The West does not need, as it did in the immediate post-war era, a pool of unskilled labour on its doorstep. As economies move from the era of industrial capitalism into the era of global capitalism, businesses move their plants to other countries in search of the cheapest possible unskilled labour. But where they do need unskilled labour domestically,

*First published in CARF, no. 57, August–September 2000.

Race & Class
Copyright © 2001 Institute of Race Relations
Vol. 42(3): 87–100 [0306-3968(200101)42:3; 87–100; 016115]

in the seasonal agricultural sector and the fluid service sector, they still require such labour to be temporary and cheap. And the rightless and the illegals fit the bill nicely.

Ironically, it is also globalism, with its demand for free markets and unfettered conditions of trade, which is eroding the distinction all over the world between the economic and the political realm. The nation state, particularly in the Third World and the eastern bloc, is the agent of global capital. It is capital which decides what to produce where, what to grow where, and how. And, through its aid and development agencies like the World Bank and International Monetary Fund and international trade agreements (such as GATT and NAFTA) and institutions like the WTO, it holds the poorer regimes in hock, and then insists that they accept austerity measures, through so-called Structural Adjustment Programmes that dictate drastic cuts in public spending, to pull them back from bankruptcy. The result is massive pauperisation, the erosion of educational, social and welfare provisions, the end of training and enterprise. There simply is no indigenous growth possible any longer, there is no future to look forward to which is not tied up with foreign powers and foreign capital. Hence resistance to economic immiseration is inseparable from resistance to political persecution. The economic migrant is also the political refugee.

That's a totally different world order from the one in which the politically persecuted refugee was defined in the UN Convention of 1951. Then, the political refugee was being defined in terms of the shame created by the annihilation of Europe's Jews and the fear engendered by Communist totalitarianism. But, already, a new category of political refugee was emerging in the newly independent states of the ex-colonies.

Colonialism and refugees
During the colonial period, Britain had collapsed diverse tribes, nationalities, ethnic groups and other geographical entities into unitary states for the purposes of easier administration and economic exploitation. In the first flush of independence, these countries, ruled by progressive nationalist governments, attempted economic policies which they hoped would give them a measure of self-sufficiency and instituted educational and training schemes which would further their national aspirations. But, as the West's neo-colonial project began to displace indigenous economic development, the nationalism which had cohered the state from independence began to give way to ethnic and communal divisions. And governments turned to using the trappings of democracy, especially the voting system, to establish authoritarian, majoritarian states, which systematically discriminated against and persecuted minority groups such as Ibos in Nigeria, Tamils in Ceylon and Asians in Kenya and Uganda.

At first, these politically persecuted refugees were economically 'invisible'. In the immediate post-war period of the 1950s and 1960s, when Britain needed all the labour it could lay its hands on, it made no distinction between economic migrants and political refugees. It did not matter that the Punjabis were fleeing the political fall-out of Partition, what mattered was that the factories of Southall needed their labour. Political refugees and economic migrants were all the same: they were labour.

Then, as Britain began to need less and less labour and its doors began to close, the claims of the persecuted came to be measured against the yardstick of economic pragmatism. The 'Kenyan Asian' episode of 1968, when Asians with British passports expelled by Kenya were refused automatic right of entry to Britain, indeed showed up the racism of Britain's immigration controls. But it was also the first clear indicator of Britain putting its economic interests before those of the politically persecuted – even when they were its own citizens. The definitions, in other words, of political refugee and economic migrant became interchangeable. So that, just four years later, British Asians from Uganda were deemed acceptable as political refugees not only because Amin gave Britain little choice, but also because they, unlike the Kenyan Asians, belonged by and large to the entrepreneurial class and could contribute to Britain's coffers. 'British', 'alien', 'political', 'economic', 'bogus', 'bona fide' – governments choose their terminology as suits their larger economic, political or ideological purpose.

Roma – the outcasts of Europe
Nothing makes this clearer than the contemporary example of the Roma from eastern Europe. In many ways, their experience in the countries of the former Soviet empire half a century ago parallels that of the minority groups displaced from newly independent states of the British empire. During the Communist era of centralisation, minority cultures and ethnic differences were suppressed. The Roma, although not allowed cultural expression and freedom of movement were, at least, part of the citizenry, an underclass maybe, but still part of a system. With the collapse of Communism, however, they became outcasts – without employment, without access to full rights, discriminated against by state agencies and persecuted by untamed populist racial terror. By any yardstick – ethnic, racial, economic, political – the Roma are a persecuted group like the Jews were earlier. And yet, when they seek refuge in western Europe, we reject them for the same reason that caused them to flee their country in the first place, that their culture and philosophy put them outside the pale of western European society. Once the underclass of Communist totalitarianism, they are today the outcasts of western democracy.

Life or livelihood
Equally, the refugees who come from the Balkans are those who have been displaced from their homes by Star Wars, waged ostensibly to save them from genocide, but in the event – because of the refusal to put troops on the ground – leading to the indiscriminate devastation of their country and, therefore, their displacement. The choice for those who face genocide appears to be either life or livelihood, but not both. And if they manage to get away with their lives and come over here, they are denied a livelihood, denied the dignity of work, and are stigmatised as beggars and scroungers, marked out this time not by the colour of their skin but by the worth of their vouchers.

As global capitalism spreads like an oil slick all over the world and cold war ideological rivalries collapse, nation states in both the former 'black' colonies of the Third World and the former 'red' colonies of the eastern bloc are beginning to break up. While giant corporations, richer than whole continents and more powerful than nation states, try to cohere the world economically, more and more people are being displaced from their countries and their homes. Some countries are being economically devastated, in others there is genocide; some countries have old-style communal wars, in others, new racisms are being unleashed. Political and economic categories have collapsed into each other, culture is becoming homogenised the world over and, increasingly, the values we live by are the values of the market place.

Globalisation reduces all human activity to the binary of buying and selling, and commercialises human relationships. So that we judge our duties and responsibilities to others not by what is owed to them, but by what it costs us. Even the wars we enter to preserve civilisation from descending into barbarism are depersonalised wars which do not involve us personally. We do not put our lives on the line for the values we hold. So that the victims of war are not – even as an extension of the values we fought for – any longer our concern.

For asylum seekers, against globalism
Globalisation fragments our consciousness and casts us into individual, single issue struggles which might bring about piecemeal reform, but not radical change. That is why it is essential that we see how each struggle – whether against institutional racism, asylum laws, arms sales or unequal trade agreements – connects with the other within the overall campaign against globalism. So that, even when we agree with the free marketeers that asylum seekers should be allowed to work, we do so not because a free labour market is an imperative of globalism, but because it is globalism that deprived them of their livelihoods in the first place. Our fight should be for the asylum seekers and therefore against globalism.

By the same token, any human rights convention that does not guarantee asylum seekers the right to a livelihood is irrelevant to the condition of our times.

A. SIVANANDAN

US

The constitutionalisation of racism: the *Hirabayashi* and *Korematsu* decisions

There is a myth, which is part of our social culture, that the Supreme Court is always the dispenser of justice. If it is the Constitution which outlines the rights explicitly retained by individuals in the Bill of Rights, it is the Supreme Court which upholds the Constitution. It is the arbiter of the constitutionality of federal government actions, the arbiter of competing constitutional interests, and the arbiter of conflicts between the exercise of government prerogative and the maintenance of individual rights. Yet, at certain crucial points, in matters of race, and despite the supposedly impartial, impersonal processes of judicial reasoning, it has been shown to be as much a prisoner of its times as any other social institution. It has unequivocally failed its own standards. This was the lesson to be drawn from two landmark cases, of 1943 and 1944 respectively, *Hirabayashi v. The United States* and *Korematsu v. The United States*.

To briefly restate the facts. In the wake of the Japanese attack on Pearl Harbor on 7 December 1941, President Roosevelt issued Executive Order No. 9066 on 19 February 1942 which granted authority to the military commander of the Western Defense Command to issue such orders as necessary for the defence of the nation. Under this authorisation, the commander, Lieutenant General J. L. DeWitt, issued an order requiring all people of Japanese ancestry within designated military areas on the west coast to be within their place of residence between the hours of 8 pm and 6 am. In *Hirabayashi*, the petitioner, an American citizen, challenged this order as unconstitutionally discriminating against citizens of Japanese ancestry in violation of the Fifth Amendment. On 21 March 1942, a second order was issued that all persons of Japanese ancestry be excluded from designated west coast military areas after 9 May 1942. In *Korematsu*, the petitioner, also an American citizen, challenged the constitutionality of that order.[1]

Why engage in an analysis of these cases? To put it simply, they illustrate constitutional failure. The decisions in these cases cannot be justified on constitutional, sociological or (legal) philosophical grounds. One of the purposes of the Bill of Rights and the Supreme Court is to protect the civil liberties of individuals in times of social crisis. In times of panic or emergency, when the rights of individuals are most likely to be trampled, it is then that the purpose and the protections of the Bill of Rights and its ultimate interpreter, the Supreme Court, should come into play. This did not happen in *Hirabayashi* and *Korematsu*. There was a constitutional breakdown. Given the facts of the case: the common, and documented, knowledge that, prior to the war's onset, people of Japanese descent, even United States citizens, faced widespread racial discrimination and hatred; that there was no positive evidence that Japanese-Americans had or would engage in acts of espionage and sabotage; that German-Americans and Italian-Americans faced no similar deprivations of civil liberties; that a constitutional history existed which recognised the heightened likelihood of civil rights infringements in times of emergencies; and the existence of an analytic framework in our constitutional jurisprudence for balancing compelling state and individual interests, then the Court's role in reviewing the acts of the government for their constitutionality takes on heightened importance. Instead, the Court abdicated its duties and was carried along by the racial hatred (public opinion) of the time. In examining *Hirabayashi* and *Korematsu*, I will look at how the institutional respectability and legitimacy of the Supreme Court, combined with the rhetoric of 'constitutionality' (which we are socialised to equate with justice), can legitimise tyranny and racism. Legitimate constitutional jurisprudence was manipulated to justify racial hatred. These cases are examples of how the Supreme Court did, and can, constitutionalise injustice, constitutionalise racism.

These decisions were contrary to the jurisprudence of the time and to well-established constitutional standards for deciding conflicts between a compelling state interest[2] and individual liberties. The Court sanctioned and facilitated the racial hysteria of the day and the unconstitutional deprivation of equal protection and due process from people of Japanese descent. The cases are constitutionally problematic. Is all that the Court says constitutional? Can the Court ever render an unconstitutional decision? These are just a couple of the questions which these decisions raise.

Laws or other state action may negatively, yet constitutionally, impact the civil liberties of individuals. The Court's decisions to deny the constitutional claims of the petitioners in favour of the government's claims of necessity are not what is disturbing. What is disturbing is its reasoning in light of the facts and available record. The Court, rather than applying constitutional standards to known facts and social circumstances (on which the dissenting opinion of Justice Frank Murphy was based in *Korematsu*), relied on the conclusions and the

openly racist opinions of Lieutenant General DeWitt. It allowed itself
to be consumed by the racial hysteria of the time and rendered a decision which reflected nothing more than the animosity felt towards US
citizens of Japanese descent and resident Japanese aliens in the aftermath of the bombing of Pearl Harbor. No factual evidence existed
which indicated that Japanese-Americans were more predisposed to
espionage and sabotage than anyone else[3] and that such a constitutional infringement would positively contribute towards effecting a
compelling state interest, i.e., the prevention of espionage and sabotage. Rather, the Court's decision was founded, as Justice Murphy
points out in his *Korematsu* dissent, on nothing more than a 'legaliza-
tion of racism'.[4]

* * *

Prior to *Hirabayashi*, the most recent enunciation of the judicial standard of review for race-based legislative classifications was in *Skinner
v. Oklahoma*.[5] In *Skinner,* Justice William Douglas penned the term
'strict scrutiny' as the standard of review for racially based legislative
classifications. The *Skinner* decision reflected the forty-six year evolution of this standard from the minimal 'reasonableness' standard of
Plessy v. Ferguson[6] (1896), i.e., 'reasonable . . . to the promotion . . .
and preservation of the public peace and good order' which was used
to uphold racial segregation in public transportation.[7] In the middle
of this evolution of a more rigorous test for the constitutionality of
racial classifications, how did the Court come to the *Hirabayashi* and
Korematsu decisions? The legislative actions fail the test for constitutionality, even if analysed under *Plessy*'s minimal and constitutionally
archaic 'reasonableness' standard, because the facts do not show that
the state action would have effected a compelling state interest.

In *Hirabayashi,* Justice Harlan Stone states that 'legislative classifi-
cation . . . based on race alone has often been found to be a denial of
equal protection'.[8] The problem is that the Court enunciates, and
later in *Korematsu* refines, this high standard of strict and rigid scrutiny
and then claims the facts (which it refused to consider) of *Hirabayashi*
and *Korematsu* meet those standards. 'It should be noted, to begin with,
that all legal restrictions which curtail the civil rights of a single racial
group are immediately suspect. That is not to say that all such restrictions are unconstitutional. It is to say that courts must subject them to
the most rigid scrutiny.'[9] The curfew and evacuation orders in fact bore
no relation to diminishing the threat from espionage and sabotage, as
was documented in Murphy's *Korematsu* dissent. So how are these
decisions to be explained?

One flaw with the Court's reasoning in *Hirabayashi* is revealed by
asking why a similar curfew was not established for those Americans

of German and Italian ancestry on the east coast?[10] Given the US's focus on the war in Europe, and that German U-Boats frequently sank cargo ships within sight of the US mainland, why were there were no similar orders affecting citizens, or even aliens, of German and Italian ancestry living on the east coast? But their European ancestry meant that German-Americans and Italian-Americans were simply seen as Americans. The Japanese were another story. Racially 'different' and sparking eugenic fears of the Yellow Peril[11] in the Euro-American population, the Japanese, even American born, were, despite their efforts, not allowed to integrate into American society. The insularity forced on the Japanese through racial discrimination was to be their curse and the cause of much of General DeWitt's paranoia regarding their presence on the west coast. It was this basic racial hatred and forced social segregation that lay at the bottom of the curfew order.

The *Hirabayashi* Court commenced justifying the reasonableness, and hence constitutionality, of the curfew order on the ground that Articles I and II of the Constitution grant the legislative and executive branches broad power to wage war. Second, it claimed constitutional justification for the delegation of those powers to the military, in that military commanders have expert knowledge of the war-time environment and logistics, and have the expertise successfully to wage war. Third, given the executive and legislative power to wage war, the Court felt it could not interject its view as to what would constitute the military's reasonable execution of those delegated powers. The question, then, is whether or not the curfew restriction was constitutional as an emergency war measure. Thus, 'it is not for any court to sit in review of the wisdom of their [the military's] actions or substitute its judgment for theirs'.[12] But, while it is true that the state is justified in using all its power to preserve itself, it would not have been unreasonable for the Court at least to review the connection between the facts and the rationale and whether there was a reasonable link between them and the curfew order. Besides, the Court cited no authority for the proclaimed inappropriateness of its reviewing military action or judgement. Moreover, this military decision was not a strictly or purely military one *per se*, since the object of it was a civilian population. Martial law had not been declared, so civilian society was not a theatre of operations but, rather, still governed by the civil authorities.

There is ample support for the proposition that the Court, in time of war, is constitutionally able to review and comment on the constitutionality of government acts. In *Ex Parte Milligan* (1866),[13] also arising from a state-of-war deprivation of constitutional rights, the Court stated that 'the constitution . . . is a law for rulers and people equally in time of war'. *Milligan* points out that, in the absence of martial law, in an area that is not actually a theatre of operations, and where the courts and civil government are still intact, constitutional rights have to be observed. Yet the Court claimed in *Hirabayashi* that it could not sit in review of an executive and legislative decision to enact a curfew that only affected those (indeed was only intended for those) of a particular race. But it is precisely at times like the aftermath of Pearl Harbor, when the rights of individuals are most likely to be trampled (such a crisis may serve as an excuse for racial oppression), that the Court should be prepared to pass judgment on the constitutionality of governmental acts. Particularly during times of war or civil commotion, individual constitutional rights need, and should receive, the watchful care of those entrusted with the guardianship of the Constitution and laws. According to *Milligan*, 'If in time of war a commander with the approval of the executive can substitute military force for and to the exclusion of laws . . . then republican government is a failure.'

I pose this hypothetical to the Court. What if General DeWitt had decided that the only way effectively to deal with this enemy within our midst, this 'potential fifth column',[14] was to execute all those of Japanese ancestry? Would the Court have still considered itself unable to pass judgment on the military's decision? Would such a proclamation have been constitutional under the federal government's War Powers?

In fact, the proclamations were nothing more than a racial lashing-out. In *Hirabayashi,* the Court accepted the hypotheses, fears and biases of General DeWitt as fact and a reasonable basis for his judgement that the proclamations were necessary for national preservation, even in the face of evidence which exposed the racism and illegitimacy of those reasons. The Court accepted his racism as the reasonable judgement that it could not constitutionally review, despite having at its disposal transcripts of the congressional committee hearings at which he gave his 'reasons' for the curfew. The Court had information that General DeWitt did not base his proclamation on military judgement but on his personal feelings and on the racism of the local white business community, which saw the war as an opportunity to be rid of its Japanese-American competitors.

What then was the 'ample ground that a reasonably prudent man had for choosing the measures' that DeWitt did for our nation's defence?[15] DeWitt made his decision, as expressed in his 'Final report'[16] on an 'erroneous assumption of racial guilt rather than bona fide military necessity'.[17] Given that Murphy cited the 'Final report' in his *Korematsu* dissent, one must assume either that the Court's majority did not also have it (unlikely) or that it chose to ignore it. What it ignored were facts which showed no military necessity behind the proclamations. The proclamations were the child of racial animosity. But even if the report had not been available for *Hirabayashi,* DeWitt's testimony before the House Naval Affairs Sub-Committee was. Here he stated that all Japanese 'are a dangerous element', that 'I don't want any of them here', 'It makes no difference if he is an American citizen, he's still Japanese', 'We must worry about the Japanese until he is wiped off the map'. This testimony was given in April 1943 and was available to the *Hirabayashi* Court which argued and decided in May and June of 1943. DeWitt's decisions were not based on military grounds but 'questionable racial and sociological grounds', something that, Murphy pointed out, is 'not ordinarily within the realm of military judgment'. DeWitt, in the 'Final report', based his decisions on the claim that those of Japanese ancestry were 'a large unassimilated tightly knit racial group bound to an enemy nation by strong ties of race, culture, custom and religion'.

DeWitt cited the dual citizenship of the Japanese as another indicator of their disloyalty. In the past, Japan, as allowed by international law, had claimed as citizens all those born of Japanese nationals, wherever located. This practice ended, however, in 1925. Japanese language schools were also cited as evidence of possible disloyalty. But Murphy argued that there had been various foreign language schools in the US for generations, without their existence being considered grounds for racial discrimination or disloyalty. Finally, DeWitt claimed that these individuals 'deliberately reside adjacent to strategic points', thus enabling them to commit sabotage on a mass scale, overlooking the fact that, in Murphy's words, 'the geographic pattern of the Japanese population was fixed years ago based on economic, social, and soil conditions'. It was economic and social discrimination faced by those of Japanese ancestry which resulted in their concentration near their initial points of entry on the Pacific coast.[18] It was also charged, falsely, that persons of Japanese ancestry were responsible for three incidents of shelling on the Pacific coast.[19] These incidents occurred, however, in September, 1942, after the Japanese had been removed from their homes and placed in concentration camps.[20] In fact, not one person of Japanese ancestry was ever accused or convicted of espionage or sabotage. Probably the only statement of fact made by DeWitt concerned the necessity of protective custody since 'the general public was ready to take matters into its own hands'.[21] What happened on the west coast in the aftermath of Pearl Harbor was racist mob rule. Reason and law were replaced by hatred and vigilantism in a racially charged environment that saw a general outpouring of violence towards anyone who was not white.[22]

Murphy saw what the rest of the Court apparently could not, that:

> the main reasons relied upon . . . do not prove a reasonable relation between the characteristics of Japanese-Americans and the dangers of invasion, sabotage, and espionage. The reasons appear instead to

be an accumulation of misinformation, half truths, and insinuations that for years have been directed against Japanese-Americans by people with racial and economic prejudices . . . people who have been the foremost advocates of the evacuation.

It was not only General DeWitt who was eager to see the Japanese removed but also 'special interest groups were extremely active in applying pressure for mass evacuation'. A spokesman for the Salinas Vegetable Grower-Shipper Association freely admitted to 'wanting to get rid of the Japs for selfish reasons'. 'It's a question of whether the white man lives on the Pacific coast or the brown man.'[23] He complained that Japanese undersold the white man because they worked their women and children, while the white man had to pay wages for help. 'If all the Japs were removed tomorrow we'd never miss them in two weeks because the white farmers can take over and produce everything the Jap grows. And we don't want them back when the war ends either.'

The Court admitted that social, economic and political conditions – denial of naturalised citizenship, prevention of land ownership, anti-miscegenation laws – had resulted in the insularity of the Japanese and prevented their assimilation, but then cited this insularity as a rational basis for suspicion of them. Justice Stone claimed that not all people of Japanese ancestry living on the west coast were a security risk but that the broad curfew order was justifiable since the Court was rushed by military necessity. In his view, hearings to see who was and was not attached to Japan would be too cumbersome, and he cited the potential for espionage and sabotage. Yet hearings were held of German aliens living in Great Britain at the beginning of the war, in which 74,000 were processed within six months.[24] While the number of Japanese-Americans living on the west coast (70,000) was deemed too great (there were a total of 112,000 people of Japanese descent), the number of hearings that would have been conducted would have been substantially fewer, since the potential for sabotage is very low among children and the elderly. Hearings to discern loyalty could have been conducted, since the evacuation did not begin until some five months after the beginning of the war. Murphy stated in *Korematsu* that, for all the talk of the necessity of immediate action, the pace of the implementation and processing of the evacuation proceeded at a leisurely pace. The Court, however, relied on General DeWitt's 'logic' that the fact that there had been no instance of sabotage was proof that it was going to happen![25]

While Stone and Douglas[26] rubber-stamped the legitimacy and constitutionality of DeWitt's proclamations, Murphy, along with Justice Owen Roberts in *Korematsu,* recognised the gravity of the case and its potential for the constitutional degeneration of civil rights. 'Few indeed', claimed Murphy, 'have been the invasions upon essential liberties which have not been accompanied by pleas of urgent necessity.' Relying on *Milligan*, he recognised the Court's duty to review and uphold constitutional boundaries. Murphy was also concerned with the social costs of the decision and what it forebode for this country: if 'we are saying that a group is unassimilatible then we have to admit that this great American experiment has failed'.[27]

However, Justice Hugo Black, writing for the majority in *Korematsu*, illustrated a racist bias towards those of Japanese ancestry. He stated that nothing short of 'apprehension' could justify the curfew or exclusion of them [people of Japanese ancestry] from the west coast. But, are feelings of apprehension, allegedly caused by no other reason than the racial dissimilarity of a group of people, a legitimate basis for depriving that group of their civil liberties? And what was the basis for this apprehension? Reliable intelligence which revealed a well-organised Japanese underground with plans for espionage and sabotage? The discovery of large arms caches? Or was it the apprehension that comes from xenophobia or racism?

*   *   *

This was the cauldron of racism into which Americans of Japanese descent found themselves plunged in the wake of Pearl Harbor. The tragedy, however, was that the supposed protector of individual rights, the Supreme Court, stood idly by. Was it racism, or a lack of courage on the Court's part? To be generous, one could conclude the latter, that the Court lacked the courage to perform its constitutional duty, to stand firm in the face of public opinion and protect the nation not from Japanese invasion but from constitutional breakdown. The Court risked the integrity of the jurisprudence which had been specifically developed to protect racial minorities from unconstitutional racial classifications by finding that the strict scrutiny standards had been met when, in fact, the evidence was to the contrary.

Can we even begin to calculate the social costs when a wink of the eye is given to a constitutional standard because of racism? As Murphy pointed out, every charge relative to race made by DeWitt was 'substantially discredited by independent studies made by experts in these matters'.[28] The military necessity which was essential to the constitutionality of an evacuation order was nothing more than 'a few intimations'. While of course there were some disloyal Japanese, so also disloyal acts had been committed by persons of German and Italian ancestry. However, individual disloyalty did not prove group disloyalty and to infer that it did 'is to deny that under our system of law individual guilt is the sole basis for deprivation of rights . . . [To] give constitutional sanction to that inference . . . is to encourage and open the door to discriminatory actions against other minority groups in the passions of tomorrow.'[29] Murphy pointed out that no adequate reason was given for the failure to treat these Americans on an individual basis as was done with people of German and Italian ancestry. There was no military necessity, the war simply provided an opportunity to exercise unfettered racism and, in the agricultural sector, deprive people of their land.

To say the least, *Hirabayashi* and *Korematsu* are constitutionally problematic decisions. While individual rights can be modified or abridged for the sake of a compelling state interest, the curtailment or denial of those rights must effectuate that state interest. Neither *Hirabayashi* or *Korematsu* meet this standard. In both cases, the Court found as constitutional a deprivation of civil liberties which had no impact on effecting a compelling state interest. This was despite having at its disposal information which showed that the proclamations were not founded on fact but, rather, on racially based fear and hate.

To claim or find that this state action was constitutional illustrates how the Court can legitimise, institutionalise and give the crushing power of the law to racial hatred.

MARK GONZALEZ

Mark Gonzalez is an assistant professor in the American Indian Studies department at the University of Minnesota-Duluth. His academic background is in legal philosophy, constitutional law and political theory, and he works primarily in the fields of constitutional law and federal Indian law.

References

1 The curfew and evacuation orders, which are the basis of *Hirabayashi* and *Korematsu* respectively, affected, without distinction, United States citizens of Japanese descent as well as non-citizen resident aliens.
2 A constitutionally legitimate end or goal which the state may pursue at the expense of individual liberties. Thus, in pursuit of effectuating a compelling state interest, a state may engage in infringements on individual civil liberties which otherwise would be considered unconstitutionally impermissible.
3 Generally, see Murphy's dissent in *Korematsu*, General Dewitt's 'Final report, Japanese evacuation from the west coast, 1942' (1943); R. Daniels, *Concentration Camps USA* (New York, Holt, Rinehart & Winston, 1972) and M. Grodzins, *Americans Betrayed* (Chicago, University of Chicago Press, 1949), which documented the voluminous outpouring of racism directed at people of Japanese descent via west coast newspapers.
4 *Korematsu*, p. 242.
5 316 US 535, 541 (1942).
6 163 US 537 (1896).
7 *Plessy*, p. 550.
8 *Hirabayashi*, p. 100.
9 *Korematsu*, p. 216.

10 Curfew orders affected German and Italian aliens but not United States citizens of German or Italian ancestry. All people of Japanese descent, including United States citizens were affected by curfew orders. All people of Japanese descent, including United States citizens, were interned. No such internment was required for those of German and Italian ancestry, including aliens.

11 R. Drinnon, *Facing West: the metaphysics of Indian hating* (Minneapolis, University of Minnesota Press, 1980).

12 *Hirabayashi*, p. 93.

13 71 US 2 (1866).

14 *Hirabayashi*, p. 90.

15 Ibid., p. 94.

16 'Final report', op. cit. While dated June 1943, it was not made public until January 1944. In it, DeWitt refers to all those of Japanese ancestry as 'subversive' and 'as belonging to an enemy race'. See *Korematsu* p. 236. However, nowhere in his report does he cite any evidence or grounds as to why these people were generally disloyal.

17 *Korematsu*, p. 235.

18 Ibid., p. 238.

19 Ibid., p. 239.

20 Ibid., p. 239.

21 Ibid., p. 238.

22 In Los Angeles in June 1943, white servicemen, particularly marines and sailors, engaged in a reign of terror of gang attacks and beatings of Mexican-American teenagers. See R. Acuna, *Occupied America: a history of Chicanos* (New York, Harper-Collins, 1988).

23 *Korematsu*, p. 239.

24 Ibid., p. 242.

25 Ibid., p. 241.

26 Just as disturbing as Stone's opinion was Douglas's concurring opinion. While generally perceived, especially in his later years, as being the Court's primary defender of civil rights, there appears no such evidence of this reputation in *Hirabayashi*. Like Stone, he refused to challenge, or review, the proclamation, stating that it may be based on factors that are 'intangible or imponderable'. See *Hirabayashi*, p. 106. What kind of rationale is this? Does it mean that we do not need facts to support decisions but can rely on gut feelings? Given his much publicised racial sensitivity, I find it surprising that he would rely on the language of a companion case, United States v. Yasui, 48 F. Supp. 40, where the court cites the 'difficulty of controlling members of an alien race' (see *Hirabayashi*, p. 106) to justify the proclamation and his refusal to address the petitioner's concerns by simply stating that the petitioner must obey the law.

27 *Hirabayashi*, p. 114.

28 *Korematsu*, p. 240.

29 Ibid., p. 240.

Book reviews

Those Bones Are Not My Child

By TONI CADE BAMBARA (New York, Pantheon Books, 1999), 676pp. $27.50.

There has never been a collective shout of 'Never Again!' about the reign of terror in the South that sustained Jim Crow segregation. Instead, the nation has willed itself not to remember the lynchings, bombings, mysterious disappearances and systematic intimidation that were such an indelible part of the American way of life for a century after slavery was abolished. Some of that history makes it into the Martin Luther King Jr Center, but almost as a footnote. The main displays – Dr King's personal items, his wife's dresses – pose little threat to the peace of mind of the visitors. After dangling their feet in the reflecting pool lapping against Dr King's sarcophagus, they may purchase from the gift shop a little piece of merchandise bearing Dr King's image. Thus is the Movement commemorated in Atlanta, once identified with *Gone with the Wind*, now 'the city too busy to hate'.

Toni Cade Bambara will have nothing to do with soothing surface appearances. In *Those Bones Are Not My Child*, a novel about the real-life abduction, mutilation and murder of more than forty African American children and young men in Atlanta in 1979–1982, she excavates 'the squalor of the truth' that lies beneath the lies of officials and the media and that consumes her characters' waking and sleeping hours like a phantasmagoric nightmare. Bambara, who lived in Atlanta at the time, spent twelve years doing intensive research into what became known as the 'Atlanta Missing and Murdered Children's Case'. The acknowledgements at the end of this volume attest to the breadth and depth of her effort, cut short by her death in 1995.

Toni Morrison, her close friend, then took on the task of reducing her 1,800 page manuscript to a dense and sometimes bewildering

Race & Class
Copyright © 2001 Institute of Race Relations
Vol. 42(3): 101–110 [0306-3968(200101)42:3; 101–110; 016118]

map of the race/class terrain of not just Atlanta, but the nation as a whole. At its centre are Zala and her estranged husband Spencer, whose 12-year-old son Sonny goes missing in July 1980 and is found nearly a year later, alive but rendered almost unidentifiable by the torment he has endured. The book chronicles their mounting sense of panic at their son's absence as shot, stabbed and strangled boys, girls and young men are found in streams, vacant lots and the Chattahoochee River. City officials insist there is no pattern to the murders, and the media bury them in back pages, if they mention them at all. From the start, 'monstrous parents, street-hustling young hoodlums . . . became the police/media version of things'. Zala, Spencer (himself a victim of post-traumatic stress) and some of his fellow Vietnam vets join in the search for Sonny and the other missing children, with the help of community activists who are routinely denounced as 'hysterical women' by the police.

The community investigators maintained the authorities 'were dragging their feet because of race; because of class; because the city, the country's third-busiest convention center, was trying to protect its image'. Forming the Committee to Stop Children's Murders (STOP), they identified six patterns to the murders: 'Klan-type slaughter, cult-type ritual murder, child-porn thrill killing, drug-related vengeance, commando/mercenary training, and overlapping combinations.' Much of the book documents the attempts of Zala, her family and friends to collect data, run down leads, separate substance from rumour, rally the community and keep sheer terror at bay. On 13 October 1980, only hours after an international white supremacist convention led by convicted bomber J. B. Stoner had adjourned in near-by Cobb County, a day care centre was blown up in Atlanta, killing four children and their teacher. With the national spotlight finally on the city, the authorities hastened to attribute the tragedy to a faulty boiler.

Eight months later, as the disappearances and bodies piled up and evidence pointed to Klan involvement and the existence of a child-porn ring, police arrested an African American 'lone wolf' as the killer, 23-year-old video cameraman, Wayne Williams. 'Until a Black man was collared, it was unacceptable to speak of hate.' Williams was convicted on two counts of murder in February 1982 and remains in prison today. The disappearances did not stop with his arrest, although that is what the people were told. 'The terror is over, the authorities say. The horror is past, they repeat every day . . . You've good reason to know that the official line is a lie.'

Those Bones Are Not My Child is not easy to read. It takes considerable concentration to piece together the fragments of information unearthed by the searchers (Bambara among them), yet wilfully overlooked by the authorities. But the book works on so many levels that its rewards are prodigious. Intertwined with the story of the Atlanta

Child Murders is the ugly saga of white supremacy's long imperium, with allusions to the destruction of 'Black Wall Street' by white mobs in Tulsa, Oklahoma, Klan and militia attacks, the Tuskegee experiment, the Freedom Summer murders, the Orangeburg Massacre, Cointelpro, the FBI's war against Black elected officials, and the myriad ways the Movement was co-opted, derailed and rolled back.

The cumulative force of Bambara's final work batters against the 'overwhelming, all-consuming, thoroughly compelling desire of the American people not to know'. Her penetrating analysis of how that longing not to know translates into acquiescence, collusion and the perpetuation of a racist system is as relevant to the two dozen suspicious 'suicides' of African American men in Mississippi jails in the late 1980s and early 1990s, and the more than two hundred suspicious conflagrations of Black southern churches between 1995 and 1997, as it is to the Atlanta murders. With so much that is still mired in racism and deceit, her truth-telling and moral urgency are profoundly missed.

Boston, MA   NANCY MURRAY

With Liberty for Some: 500 years of imprisonment in America

By SCOTT CHRISTIANSON (Illinois, Northeastern University Press, 1998), 394pp.

Imagine welcoming strangers into your home or community with warmth and loving-kindness. Showered with food, shelter and clothing, these guests are provided with the basic necessities for survival as foreigners: a new way of life is introduced complete with a different language and culture. In exchange for such hospitality, the hosts are slandered, robbed and slaughtered in reckless abandon. Should there be any survivors, prison camps (reservations) are constructed for their long-term confinement.

The first political prisoners in the United States were Native Americans. One of the questions in the preface of *With Liberty for Some* is the role of imprisonment in this country. The Boston house of correction was erected in 1632 to punish offenders and deter others, at a time when there were less than forty houses in the community. Various counties in the eastern states constructed buildings to confine petty theft offenders, unruly servants and runaway slaves. Scott Christianson does an excellent job in identifying the multiple purposes of confinement, while presenting the negative impact of imprisonment on families and communities. A primary purpose is human deprivation, even though such deprivation produces emotional scars for generations.

Chattel slavery promoted racial hatred and exploitation of poor and non-white folks. This 'peculiar' institution prospered by kidnapping African people and transporting them in slave vessels to America. The plight of nearly 2 million human beings in chains today, throughout the United States, originated with ships sailing the ocean from Africa. Penal slavery replaced chattel slavery by virtue of the Civil War, the 13th Amendment and an intricate plan to continue the bondage of Africans in America. Remnants of slavery are exhibited at the southern prison farms located in Angola (Louisiana), Parchman (Mississippi) and Tucker (Arkansas). Although Christianson states that prisons were not built exclusively for blacks, a high percentage of current prisoners are descendants of former slaves.

Two different prison systems (Auburn and Eastern) were designed during the mid-nineteenth century. The Auburn (New York) policy allowed prisoners to leave their cells during specified times but prohibited interaction, while the Eastern (Pennsylvania) penitentiary confined human beings to the cell for the entire sentence. Christianson describes how both 'systems relied on silence, separation, discipline, regimentation, and industry to achieve positive human change'. Nonetheless, punishments such as the 'shower bath', buckets of icy cold water dropped upon the head of the prisoner, and the 'mad chair', an object to strap and restrain an individual, are humiliating, painful and contradictory to the promotion of rehabilitation.

Approximately 20 million human beings are released from custody annually in the United States. Many return to prison because they lack social skills and are in worse (physical, mental, financial) condition than before their original imprisonment. Christianson articulates this point by saying 'prison only made a good man bad and a bad man worse'. He examines prison construction, cost, the expense of lengthy confinement, privatisation of the industry, violence in the prison and the effectiveness of punishment versus treatment of the convicted felon. Prisons are identified as a major public safety issue, while funding for education and welfare has decreased.

Those confined in the major penal institutions have to know the slang and learn to monitor the activity in the yard. It is refreshing to read about the 'code' at the beginning of the chapter on 'doing time' because the importance of this code within the prison subculture needs to be highlighted. This unwritten set of laws may vary from prison to prison throughout the country, but the basic tenets remain: mind your own business, don't talk to the authorities and maintain respect among your peers. It was designed by and for prisoners and is often contrary to the goals and objectives of the authorities. One must never underestimate the importance of the code, for nonadherence could be fatal.

Scott Christianson does raise and address some provoking questions in this comprehensive examination of the criminal justice system. His book provides us with the opportunity to ignite a debate that requires courage and honest discussion. In particular, we, as a society, need to understand the story of slavery and its relationship to the social dilemma that more black youth are in prison than college. The voices in the dungeons need to roar loud enough to invoke the pugnacious spirit of the African ancestors. *A luta continua*!

Bay State Center, Norfolk, MA   ARNOLD L. KING
[email: chrisl@cbinet.com]

Claudia Jones: a life in exile

By MARIKA SHERWOOD (London, Lawrence and Wishart, 1999), 256pp. £13.99.

She founded two of black Britain's key institutions – its carnival and its press. She galvanised protest against the first New Commonwealth Immigration Act in 1962. Yet, for almost two decades, Trinidadian-born Claudia Jones who, as a victim of US anti-communism, was forced into exile in Britain in 1955 where she died in 1964 and who was a huge figure in the development of Britain's black community, remained almost unknown. Attempts were made in the 1980s to compensate for this neglect with a book by Buzz Johnson (mainly about her thirty-three years in the US, called *'I Think of my Mother'*, published by Karia) and a pamphlet by Camden Black Sisters (*Claudia Jones, 1915–1964*).

In 1996, Marika Sherwood, a self-taught historian of Black British history, realising that the generation that had been politically active with Claudia was dying off, urged all those who had known and worked with her to pool their memories at a symposium. And, from such rich recollections and contributions, from, for example, Colin Prescod (whose mother Pearl had sung at events organised by Claudia) and Donald Hinds (who had worked on Claudia's paper), and her own painstaking research in numerous archives, has this book been woven. It traces Claudia's activities in her nine years of exile in Britain, with chapters on how she settled down in England, her relationship with the Communist Party, the creation of the *West Indian Gazette*, the development of carnival, her death and legacy.

From the vantage point of today's posture politics, her achievements were, indeed, remarkable. She was able to fuse the burgeoning cultural and political black movements in Britain, to link Asian workers with West Indians, to combine anti-racism with movements for colonial freedom.

She inspired people. 'She made you fearless. There was some quality in Claudia that gave you the impetus and a feeling that you could win', recalled Pearl Connor. Other contemporaries speak of her vitality, organising capacity, tenacity and commitment in the face of debilitating illnesses and constant anxieties about money. Nor was she a dour party hack. 'Militant for her cause, she was also gracious in her relationships. The Lioness could disagree like an angel', wrote George Lamming in the memorial issue of the *Gazette*. The angel had attracted to 'her cause' a younger generation of West Indians – which included, apart from Lamming, Andrew Salkey, Jan Carew and John La Rose.

There are essentially two stories about Claudia Jones – one which is here, one which is not. The first is the account of her life and contribution to black struggle in Britain. The second, which really explains the first, the story of why she got written out of its history, can only be gleaned by reading between the lines. Her stand against racism put her at odds with protectionist workerism; the range of her internationalism, including support for China and Vietnam, put her under suspicion from the CPGB; her confidence and style were derided as American and unwomanly by the small-minded; and, for the individualistic libertarians of the early black power movement, her brand of dedicated politics smacked of an unwelcome discipline.

A feminist before feminism, a black leader before the acceptance of black autonomy, a questioner of Soviet strictures before it was fashionable, no one, it seems, save Abhimanyu Manchanda – her one-time lover, friend and co-worker, who became associated with the small Maoist wing of British Marxist politics – tried to keep her memory alive after her sudden death at the age of 49.

If I have had to speculate here, it is because Marika Sherwood refuses to do so. But then, she is a hunter-gatherer of everything from footnotes, minutes, press reports and intelligence files to handbills, memorabilia and personal remembrances. She writes as a kind of dispassionate go-between, bringing the world of Robeson concerts at St Pancras, Brixton office politics and south Hampstead bedsit land in the 1950s and 1960s back to the reader of today. Her writing is packed with the facts and personal opinions that she has gleaned, but she intrudes almost no analysis of her own. Nor does she often widen the aperture of her camera eye to situate Claudia in the wider world. Ironically, though her book is magnificent as reclamation and historical record, it lacks the vitality that she so admires in her subject. Hopefully, the volume of Claudia's collected writings now being prepared for publication by Carole Boyce Davis, Diane Langford and Alrick Cambridge (provisionally entitled *Claudia Jones: beyond containment*) will serve as the necessary complement.

Institute of Race Relations   JENNY BOURNE

Deadly Dreams: opium and the Arrow war in China 1856–1860

By J. Y. WONG (Cambridge, Cambridge University Press, 1998), 542pp. £50.00.

On 8 October 1856, the Chinese crew of the *lorcha, Arrow*, were arrested by the Chinese authorities on suspicion of involvement in piracy. This minor incident, hardly worth even a footnote in the history books, was to prove the excuse for the second opium war. For a second time, now in alliance with the French, the British were to attempt to incorporate the Manchu empire within their own informal empire. China was to be subordinated to Britain in the same fashion as South America, formally independent, but, nevertheless, run for the benefit of the British. A crucial factor in this was the opium trade.

The British empire was at this time the biggest drug pusher the world has ever seen. A matter of some significance, one would have thought, but obviously not, because it is ignored or downplayed in book after book. Indeed, when one comes to look at western histories of the second opium war, one of the most interesting facts is the way they actually avoid the subject of opium and go out of their way to find other motives. Even Douglas Hurd, the former Tory foreign secretary, has produced a volume exploring what he amusingly calls 'the Anglo-Chinese confusion'.

Of course, interpretations of the war to a considerable extent depend on attitudes towards the British empire. Was it the empire on which the sun never set? Or on which the blood never dried? If the latter, then the second opium war is easily seen for what it really was. If the former, then excuses and alibis have to be found, no matter how implausible, because British gentlemen just do not behave like this. The alternative is unthinkable: the empire-builders were little better than gangsters and often worse. Western historians are united in rejecting this scenario.

This benign consensus is no longer tenable, however, because John Wong's marvellous study, *Deadly Dreams*, scatters it to the winds. In a work of great scholarship that has all the excitement of a detective story, Wong reveals the nature of the crime, establishes the motive and identifies those responsible. This was, he conclusively shows, a war about 'big money and narcotics'.

Let us start with the *Arrow* affair. Although it was Chinese owned and crewed, the vessel was registered in Hong Kong with, nominally, a British captain. The pretext for the British attack on the Chinese was the claim that, when arresting the *lorcha*'s crew, the Chinese police had lowered and consequently dishonoured the Union Jack. Their failure even to admit to this, let alone apologise for it, required punishment that was best administered by the Royal Navy. As Wong shows, it is extremely unlikely that the Union Jack was flying on the *Arrow*, because it was never flown when ships were at anchor, but only when under way. There was certainly no intention on the part of the Chinese of provoking an incident, but every reason to believe that the British were looking for a pretext for armed confrontation. The problem for apologists for the empire was that the men on the spot, Harry Parkes, consul at Canton, and Sir John Bowring, governor of Hong Kong, picked such a flimsy pretext. This was to cause the British government some embarrassing moments. It was quickly discovered, for example, that the *Arrow*'s Hong Kong registration had lapsed and, later on, that the vessel had indeed been involved in piracy. These were not the real issues.

As Wong shows, the *Arrow* affair was a clumsily manufactured pretext for, and not the cause of, war. The British government had already decided that the terms of the Treaty of Nanking, imposed after the first opium war, were not good enough and that a new settlement was necessary. China had to be opened up and the opium trade legalised whether the Manchu government liked it or not. This was the cause of the war.

Wong spends considerable time exploring what he describes as Britain's 'liberal conscience', and this was of some moment because it was to bring Palmerston's government down and force a general election. There was a widespread feeling in parliament that the conduct of Bowring, in particular, had been ill-advised at best and in breach of international law at worst. The shelling of Canton seemed a disproportionate response if the *Arrow* affair was what was really at stake. Indeed, when Palmerston invited the attorney-general, Richard Bethell, to advise the cabinet, Bethell made it clear that a serious case could be made against the British government and that, if it were not for his position as a member of the government, he would have supported a vote of censure himself. After defeat in the Commons, Palmerston dissolved parliament and fought a fiercely jingoistic campaign that triumphantly returned him to office.

While Wong is quite right to emphasise the importance of the 'liberal conscience' in nineteenth-century Britain, he underestimates its moral flexibility. Bowring, the governor of Hong Kong and the instigator of the war, was a leading liberal intellectual with a European reputation, while Lord Elgin, the man sent out as plenipotentiary to actually conduct the war, was similarly a well-known liberal figure, the architect of Canadian self-government. Moreover, a number of those liberals who had voted against Palmerston in the censure campaign accepted office after the general election in his new government and helped wage the war. Sidney Herbert, Edward Cardwell, Lord John Russell, and even William Gladstone, all rallied to the cause.

What of the role of the opium trade? Wong successfully establishes its crucial importance for the British empire and as a motive for war with China. He writes:

The present research shows that opium was not just helping to balance the United Kingdom's trade with China. It generated huge profits; it funded imperial expansion and maintenance in India; it provided the much needed silver to develop the trading network among the countries bordering on the Indian Ocean; it assisted the growth of Bombay and other Indian cities; it enabled the United Kingdom to obtain tea and silk from China for very little initial cost, and it was a great help in the United Kingdom's global balance of payments.

In addition, this China trade was a channel of remittance from India to London . . . Greenberg noticed a flow of goods from India to China and from China to the United Kingdom. . . . His observation, however, has barely scratched the surface of what were significant economic interests to India and to the United Kingdom, all of which depended to a large extent on . . . opium.

The point is established well beyond reasonable doubt.

The second and third opium wars were to see Anglo-French forces fight their way to Beijing, loot and burn the Emperor's Summer Palace and impose the humiliating Treaty of Tientsin. The Manchus had been brought to heel and the lucrative opium trade was safeguarded. Another volume, carrying the story forward, would be wonderful, but we must be content with Wong's definitive account of the causes of the war.

Bath Spa University College   JOHN NEWSINGER

Iraq under siege: the deadly impact of sanctions and war

Edited by ANTHONY ARNOVE (London, Pluto Press and Boston, South End Press, 2000), 216pp. Paper £10.99.

Iraq Under Siege is an important and impressive addition to the growing literature on the sanctions on Iraq. A fifteen-chapter, fifteen-author bonanza, the book includes items by Denis Halliday, Noam Chomsky, John Pilger, Robert Fisk and Howard Zinn. The pieces by Halliday (who resigned in protest from his position as UN Humanitarian Co-ordinator for Iraq) and Chomsky are actually transcriptions from speech, and there is a sense that the book is designed to be easily digestible, delivered in bite-size pieces (though with enough footnotes for the rigorously minded). But, on the other hand, the sheer number of essays/articles/briefings inevitably produces an impression of fragmentation.

The core of the argument against economic sanctions on Iraq is that there is a humanitarian crisis in Iraq of considerable proportions (700,000 children under five remain chronically malnourished, despite three years of the 'oil for food' programme), that the economic sanctions constitute the principal barrier to the solution of this humanitarian crisis, and that the social and economic rights of 22 million Iraqi civilians (as codified in the Universal Declaration of Human Rights, for example) are therefore being violated by the United Nations Security Council.

Rather than beginning by demonstrating that there is a humanitarian crisis, *Iraq Under Siege* first examines 'the roots of US/UK policy' (actually only US policy) and then moves on to 'Myths and realities' concerning sanctions and war. It is only in chapter 14 that we find a solid, sober documentation of the effects of sanctions by Dr Peter L. Pellett, professor of nutrition at the University of Massachusetts and participant in three UN Food and Agriculture Organisation missions to Iraq during the last decade. Incidentally, Pellett sets out some of the real reasons for the differences in death rates between the autonomous Kurdish zone in northern Iraq and the rest of the country, something officially attributed to Baghdad's sabotage of 'oil for food'. (Pellett does not mention that UNICEF, whose survey discovered the difference, also stated categorically, 'What we do know is that the difference [in mortality rates] cannot be attributed to the differing ways the Oil for Food Program is implemented in the two parts of Iraq'.)

The most useful activist essay, by Ali Abunimah and Rania Masri, on combating media spin, is chapter 6. The final chapter is taken up by Sharon Smith's rather foreshortened view of the development of the anti-sanctions movement. The most sizeable activist contribution to the book is by the sanctions-breaking group Voices in the Wilderness (US), whose briefing on 'Myths and realities' is included as a chapter, as are moving essays by Voices member George Capaccio and co-ordinator Kathy Kelly. (Kelly and Denis Halliday have been nominated for the Nobel Peace Prize by the Quaker organisation, the American Friends Service Committee.)

The economic sanctions against Iraq constitute one of the major crimes against humanity of our era, devastating the lives of millions of civilians through the use of an economic weapon of mass destruction. *Iraq Under Siege* is an urgent call to action which deserves the widest possible audience.

Voices in the Wilderness, UK   MILAN RAI